Blueprint for Computer-assisted Assessment

What role can technology play in improving the assessment of student learning?

The rapid development and integration of computer-assisted assessment (CAA) in mainstream post-compulsory educational institutions today make this an exciting and invaluable reference text. It provides a practical, research-based guide on a subject that is becoming increasingly important as the use of technology to assess student learning expands.

The book addresses both theory and practice, offering a comprehensive evaluation of many key aspects of CAA such as:

- question and test design, scoring and analysis, feedback and integration with other assessment methods;
- the role of CAA in feedback processes;
- wider use of technology to support and enhance assessment;
- technical, operational and support issues.

The authors present here a lucid, balanced analysis of the strengths and weaknesses of CAA. This text will appeal to all those involved in higher or further education who wish to model their CAA systems on the best practice available.

Joanna Bull is Director of Eduology, who provide research and consultancy for businesses and educational institutions. **Colleen McKenna** is lecturer in Academic Literacies at the University College London.

Blueprint for Computer-assisted Assessment

Joanna Bull and
Colleen McKenna

RoutledgeFalmer
Taylor & Francis Group

LONDON AND NEW YORK

First published 2004
by RoutledgeFalmer
11 New Fetter Lane, London EC4P 4EE

Simultaneously published in the USA and Canada
by RoutledgeFalmer
29 West 35th Street, New York, NY 10001

RoutledgeFalmer is an imprint of the Taylor & Francis Group

Typeset in Times by
Bookcraft Ltd, Stroud, Gloucestershire
Printed and bound in Great Britain by
TJ International Ltd, Padstow, Cornwall

British Library Cataloguing in Publication Data
A catalogue record for this book is available
from the British Library

Library of Congress Cataloging-in-Publication Data
Bull, Joanna.
    Blueprint for computer-assisted assessment /
Joanna Bull and Colleen McKenna.
       p. cm.
    Includes bibliographical references and index.
    ISBN 0–415–28703–0 – ISBN 0–415–28704–9 (pbk.)
    1. Universities and colleges–Examinations–Data processing. 2. College
students–Rating of–Data processing. 3. Examinations–Design and
construction. I. McKenna, Colleen, 1965– II. Title.

    LB2366.B87 2003
    378.1'662'0285–dc21
                                                              2003046557

ISBN 0–415–28703–0 (hbk)
ISBN 0–415–28704–9 (pbk)

For Dale and Martin

Contents

Acknowledgements

This book is a revised version of the 'Blueprint for Computer-assisted Assessment' produced as part of a Teaching and Learning Technology Programme project, the Implementation and Evaluation of Computer-assisted Assessment. The project was funded by the Higher Education Funding Council for three years between 1998 and 2001 and comprised colleagues from the Universities of Loughborough, Luton, Glasgow and Oxford Brookes.

The authors wish to thank all the project members who provided contributions, advice and guidance during the project, in particular: Carol Collins, University of Luton; Bryan Dawson, Loughborough University; Richard Francis, Oxford Brookes University; Val Martin-Revell, University of Luton; Chris Rust, Oxford Brookes University; Derek Stephens, Loughborough University; Dave Whittington, University of Glasgow and Stan Zakrzewski, University of Luton.

We would also like to acknowledge and thank colleagues who provided example questions, case studies and specific advice and guidance: Memis Acar, Loughborough University; Martin Anthony, London School of Economics; Cliff Beevers, Heriot Watt University; Valerie Boyle, Loughborough University; James Dalziel, University of Sydney; David Davies, University of Birmingham; David Edwards, Loughborough University; Paul Finlay, Loughborough University; Fiona Lamb, Loughborough University; Jane Magill, University of Glasgow; Don Mackenzie, University of Derby; David Percek, Loughborough University; Keith Pond, Loughborough University; Roger M. Smith, Loughborough University; Ruth Stubbings, Loughborough University; Roger Suthren, Oxford Brookes University; Joe Ward, Loughborough University and members of the Engineering Assessment Network.

Special thanks go to: Myles Danson, particularly for contributions about optical data technologies; Ian Hesketh for valuable advice, support and unravelling statistics and Dale Sharp for patiently and instantly providing advice and guidance on technical and operational issues.

Part of Chapter 2 (a version of the e-literacy section) first appeared in McKenna (2002). In addition, previous work presented as a discussion session at the 5th International CAA Conference was also drawn on to inform this chapter (see McKenna, 2001). Sections from Chapters 10 and 11 first appeared in McKenna and Bull (2000).

Abbreviations

CAA	computer-assisted assessment
CAL	computer-aided learning
CAT	computer adaptive test(s)
CBA	computer-based assessment
CMC	computer-mediated communication
HE	higher education
HEFC	Higher Education Funding Council
HTML	HyperText Markup Language
ICR	intelligent character reading
ID	identification
IMS	Instructional Management Systems (formerly)
IRT	item response theory
IT	information technology
MCQs	multiple-choice questions
MRQ	multiple-response questions
OCR	optical character recognition
OMR	optical mark reader(s)
PDF	Portable Document Format
QTI	Question and Test Interoperability
SCORM	Shareable Content Object Reference Model
UK	United Kingdom
US	United States
VLE	virtual learning environment(s)
VPN	Virtual Private Network
W3C	World Wide Web Consortium
XML	Extensible Markup Language

Introduction

Why an entire book on the use of computers in assessment? For a start, while computer-assisted assessment (CAA) is not exactly a new approach, over the last decade it has been developing rapidly in terms of its integration into schools, universities and other institutions; its educational and technical sophistication; and its capacity to offer elements, such as simulations and multimedia-based questions, which are not feasible with paper-based assessments. It is, therefore, quite an exciting time to take a comprehensive look at the body of work that falls under the umbrella of CAA. Additionally, there is currently much activity in two very relevant areas for CAA: assessment and learning technology. Part of what we attempt to do here is position work in CAA within the debates in both 'fields' and comment on ways in which CAA becomes a point of intersection between them. Finally, this book seeks to provide an introduction to and discussion of the main issues associated with CAA and to support its use in education. In so doing, we have imagined a diverse readership including academics, educational developers and researchers, learning technologists, computer services personnel and staff responsible for quality assurance and enhancement. For this reason, the text covers a large number of topics (ranging from question design to security procedures) and contains appendices that provide detailed practical advice.

While many practical issues are described and discussed, the book draws throughout on the emerging body of research into CAA and related work in assessment and learning technologies. Across the sector, it would appear that the emphasis on the importance of research into higher education policy and practices is growing and this area is no exception. We review a number of recent studies into the use of CAA, but we are also aware that, in common with learning technology generally, there is much more research and theorising to be done.

Technology changes rapidly and this book does not attempt to review or describe in detail specific tools or software which can be used to assess student learning. That said, through case studies and examples, we do refer to some particular CAA projects and systems in order to illustrate specific techniques and practices, such as question design, use of simulation or novel approaches to feedback. However, a key concern of this publication is to consider the pedagogical implications of introducing CAA into the curriculum, whether for formative or summative purposes. So we address, in some depth, issues of appropriateness of certain CAA methods in terms of disciplines and levels of learning and understanding; options for question and test design; the extent to which CAA imposes constraints upon teachers and learners; and ways in which it enables certain activities such as increased access to self-assessment and feedback. Like all methods, CAA has strengths and weaknesses, and we suggest throughout that CAA should be considered in conjunction with other approaches within assessment strategies. Used appropriately, CAA can be a powerful and fruitful way to enhance student learning, build new activities into assessment, and potentially release marking time.

For the purposes of this book, CAA is defined as the use of computers in the assessment of student learning. Additionally, we use the following, standard terms to classify methods of assessment:

- *Diagnostic assessment*   tests which are taken to determine a student's prior knowledge of a subject.
- *Self-assessment*   tests which are taken by students to check their understanding of particular concepts and terminology.
- *Formative assessment*   assessments which assist learning by giving feedback which indicates how the student is progressing in terms of knowledge, skills and understanding of a subject. In CAA, this often takes the form of objective questions with feedback given to the student either during or immediately after the assessment. Formative assessment may be monitored by the tutor, used purely for self-assessment, or used to contribute marks to a module grade.
- *Summative assessment*   assessments where the primary purpose is to give a quantitative grading and make a judgement about the student's achievement in a particular area. Summative assessment can include marked coursework as well as end-of-module examinations and can incorporate feedback to the student.

In practice, there may be areas of overlap between different types of assessment.

Finally, the book falls roughly into two parts, with the first eight chapters addressing educational aspects such as question and test design, scoring and analysis, feedback and integration with other assessment methods. Chapter 1 introduces CAA and briefly discusses some key pedagogical issues surrounding its use. Chapter 2 attempts to locate CAA within the contexts of assessment, generally, and emerging learning technology practices. It also addresses issues of control and empowerment. Chapters 3 to 7 consider the most common form of CAA – objective tests. An overview of different question types and associated pedagogical issues is set out, along with suggestions for writing questions. Feedback to students and staff is a potential benefit of CAA, and Chapter 5 asks what CAA can contribute to feedback processes and considers approaches to designing feedback for CAA, including predefined responses, model answers, online response to essays, and mixed-mode feedback. Chapter 6 addresses the scoring and statistical analysis of objective tests, while Chapter 7 considers the construction and integration of objective tests with other assessment methods. Practice and research which extends beyond the use of objective tests is explored in Chapter 8, including CAA-related activities involving virtual learning environments and computer-mediated communication, electronic marking of free text and the potential use of gaming techniques for assessment. The remaining chapters cover technical, operational and support areas. The range of technologies which are currently used to deliver both optical and screen-based CAA is discussed in Chapter 9, with the broader issues of planning, invigilation, security, network capacity, staff development and student support covered in Chapter 10. This chapter also suggests ways of encouraging institution-wide discussion and debate about CAA (and other assessment) practices. Chapter 11 discusses the need for and approaches to evaluating and researching CAA and suggests some themes and topics for such work.

Chapter 1

Computer-assisted assessment

This chapter defines computer-assisted assessment (CAA) and considers how and why it might be used as part of an assessment strategy. It also addresses the merits and limitations of CAA.

What is computer-assisted assessment (CAA)?

CAA is a common term for the use of computers in the assessment of student learning. The term encompasses the use of computers to deliver, mark and analyse assignments or examinations. It also includes the collation and analysis of optically captured data gathered from machines such as optical mark readers (OMR). An additional term is 'computer-based assessment' (CBA), which refers to an assessment in which the questions or tasks are delivered to a student via a computer terminal. Other terms used to describe CAA activities include computer-based testing, computerised assessment, computer-aided assessment and web-based assessment (where browsers are used to deliver tests). The term 'screen-based assessment' encompasses both web-based and computer-based assessment.

An OMR is a machine which rapidly processes paper forms by scanning the page for marks such as shaded boxes, crosses or ticks. (For example, the National Lottery uses OMR technology and many universities process student questionnaires in this way.) For assessment purposes, preprinted paper tests are taken by students using pen or pencil and fed into an OMR at rates of up to 2200 forms per hour. Exam questions must be objective and the answer sheets must be printed on special machine-readable paper.

The most common format for items delivered by CAA is objective test questions (such as multiple-choice or true/false) which require a student to choose or provide a response to a question whose correct answer is predetermined. However, there are other types of question which can be used with CAA. Chapters 3, 4 and 8 discuss question formats and design in detail.

Why use CAA?

There are many motivations for implementing CAA within a course and it is often a combination of factors which results in CAA being used either formatively or summatively with students.

Table 1.1 lists reasons why you might wish to use CAA. The list is not definitive, but may be useful in helping you to define your motivation for considering CAA.

Pedagogical issues

Is CAA appropriate?

It is important to identify clearly what you want a particular assignment, test or examination to assess prior to choosing an assessment method. The skills, abilities and knowledge which you wish your students to demonstrate in a particular assignment will probably be determined to a large extent by the learning outcomes of the course. Brown *et al.* (1997) provide a comprehensive overview of different methods of assessment (such as essays, objective tests, reports and presentations) and their strengths and weaknesses. These methods can be assessed using a range of mechanisms including, for example, tutor, peer, self and computer. Once the most appropriate method is determined, it is then possible to consider the most suitable mechanisms for delivering the assessment.

Integration with existing assessment methods and strategies

When considering CAA, it is useful to look at the types of assessment which are currently being used and evaluate whether they are effective in assessing relevant disciplinary skills and abilities. No single assessment method is able to evaluate all the skills and abilities which students are expected to develop in their courses; therefore, in order to maintain a balanced assessment profile, CAA objective tests should be used as only one of a number of assessment methods. Chapter 7 provides more detail and specific examples of matching assessment methods to learning outcomes.

Integration within course

CAA should be used within an appropriate context. Research shows that to be effective, the introduction and implementation of learning

Table 1.1 Some reasons for using CAA

> 1 To increase the frequency of assessment, thereby:
>   - motivating students to learn
>   - encouraging students to practise skills
> 2 To broaden the range of knowledge assessed
> 3 To increase feedback to students and lecturers
> 4 To extend the range of assessment methods
> 5 To increase objectivity and consistency
> 6 To decrease marking loads
> 7 To aid administrative efficiency

technology should be integrated with the structure and delivery of the course (Ehrmann, 1998). The purpose of the CAA must be apparent to students, and the relationship between the CAA and teaching sessions and other assessed work should be clearly identified.

CAA should also be appropriate for students taking the course. It is important that students are given the opportunity to practise, both with the software and the assessment method, before undertaking any summative assessments. It may be necessary to provide specific training or supporting documentation for students undertaking CAA. The majority of students in higher education develop information technology (IT) skills as part of their studies and, increasingly, they have experience of IT prior to entering university. CAA can be used to help students further develop the capacity to use IT in their subject, but it is important to guard against CAA which unintentionally assesses IT skills rather than course material. Chapter 10 discusses in detail ways of supporting students in the use of CAA.

The remainder of this section discusses a number of potential reasons for implementing CAA.

Increasing the frequency of assessment

Motivating students to learn

There is much evidence to show that assessment is the driving force behind student learning (Beevers *et al.*, 1991; Brown *et al.*, 1997). It is increasingly the case that students are becoming ever more strategic in their study habits (Kneale, 1997), and they are reluctant to undertake work which does not count towards their final grade. There is evidence that some students academically at risk fail to adopt appropriate study skills (Tait and Entwistle, 1996) in an HE environment which requires an increasing reliance on self-regulated learning (Vermunt, 1998). CAA offers the potential to make supporting material available, which may be of particular benefit to those students who require study skills and learning support. However, sometimes convincing students to undertake valuable but unassessed work can be difficult.

There are a number of strategies which could be used to motivate student learning using CAA. For example, a lecturer could include one or more of the following in an assessment profile:

- A sequence of tests taken throughout the module which students must complete in order to qualify to take the module examination. This is the strategy being adopted by the Scottish Qualifications Authority in their new Higher Still programmes.
- A series of tests which are taken at intervals throughout the module which count for a small percentage of the total grade.
- Short tests taken at the beginning of a practical class, lecture or tutorial to assess learning from previous sessions and provide feedback to students during the following teaching session.
- A test which must be taken prior to undertaking a particular assignment. The test could provide the opportunity to decide on student groups for project work, assign responsibilities for group work or assign assessment tasks.
- Self-assessment material which provides specific and timely feedback and is available 'on demand' for students to use repetitively if desired.

Encouraging students to practise disciplinary skills and abilities

CAA can also offer the opportunity to allow students to practise particular skills and work with specific areas of subject knowledge. Using CAA for self-assessment can enable and encourage students to monitor their own progress, motivate them to learn and provide them with a tool which lets them work at their own pace and level.

CAA can also offer a potentially novel learning experience for students with the advantage that computers never tire of repeating themselves, are non-judgemental, and give feedback that can be used to direct students to other learning resources, both computer- and paper-based. If self-assessment material can be designed to be interesting, informative and interactive, it may encourage students to practise and further motivate them to learn.

Broadening the range of knowledge assessed

As suggested above, the majority of CAA currently delivered in higher education uses objective tests as the format for assessments. Objective tests lend themselves well to testing a broad knowledge base within a particular discipline. In many courses, there is a body of underpinning knowledge which must be learned to enable progression during the later stages of the course (Brown *et al.*, 1997). (Chapters 3 and 4 provide further details on the use and design of objective tests.)

Different assessment methods are effective at assessing different levels, knowledge and understanding. Using a balance of assessment methods may allow a fuller range of abilities and knowledge to be assessed within a course.

Increasing feedback

Students

Students are motivated by feedback on their work. To assist in improving learning, feedback needs to be timely, given during the course rather than at the end of it. Feedback also needs to be accurate and constructive (Falchikov, 1995), and regular, formative feedback has been shown to have a marked improvement on students' overall performance on a course (Schmidt *et al.*, 1990).

CAA provides the opportunity to give students timely, accurate and constructive feedback in a specific and directed manner. Large student groups often mean that academic staff are unable to give formative feedback on student learning to the extent they may wish. CAA automates this process, allowing students to receive feedback on demand.

Computerised objective tests allow a range of feedback options, from automated feedback, denoting score and correct/incorrect responses, to individual feedback messages associated with each correct or incorrect option. CAA enables the provision of consistent (but standardised) feedback to large student groups and can be used to direct student learning by identifying and anticipating problem areas. Chapter 5 considers the role and design of feedback for CAA.

Academic staff

CAA can also provide academic staff with rapid feedback about their students' performance. Assessments which are marked automatically can offer immediate and evaluative statistical analysis allowing academics to quickly assess whether their students have understood the material being taught, both at an individual and group level. If students have misconceptions about a particular theory/concept or gaps in their knowledge, these can be identified and addressed before the end of the course or module.

CAA can also provide valuable information about the quality of the questions used in objective tests and other types of CAA. By taking into account not only student performance but also question performance, assessments can be refined to ensure that they are valid and reliable and are accurately assessing specified learning outcomes. Chapter 6 gives more details about analysing and scoring objective test questions.

Extending the range of assessment methods

It has already been suggested that different assessment methods are necessary to assess different knowledge and abilities. There is often an over-reliance on one particular method of assessment, which can lead to the same knowledge, skills and understanding being repeatedly assessed. CAA can offer the opportunity to widen the range of assessment methods and enable knowledge and understanding to be tested which might otherwise be neglected.

Additionally, through the inclusion of computer graphics, sound, animated images and video clips, CAA has the potential to offer varied, innovative assignments which extend the boundaries of paper-based assessments. It is also possible to integrate CAA with computer-aided learning (CAL) materials to provide learning and assessment materials which are self-paced and formative.

Objectivity and consistency in marking

There is much to suggest that individual markers and groups of markers can be both inconsistent and subjective in their marking (Brown *et al.*, 1997). The volume of assessments to be marked in further and higher education has increased as a result of rising student numbers and the introduction of modular systems. Students are increasingly positioned as customers by the educational system and there is, it would seem, a need to be aware of the risk of complaints and litigation (Knight,

2002b). Assessment is a key area for concern as the validity of any assessment is at risk if marking is unreliable and inconsistent. The automated marking of CAA allows consistent and objective marking to be achieved with large groups of students. The ability of CAA to provide detailed information about student and test performance allows rigorous evaluation of the assessment method, making it easier to ensure that the CAA is consistent with learning outcomes and that standards are adhered to.

Decreasing marking load

There are potentially great timesavings to be made through the automatic marking of students' work. However, it is important to recognise the investment of time which must take place in the design of the assessment and in managing its implementation. Depending on the level at which CAA is used, the timesavings achieved will vary. If an individual academic designs and delivers CAA with little or no technical support, the time invested may, in the first instance, be equal to or exceed that of the time saved by marking automatically. If there is support available from administrative or technical staff, or a source of questions for the assessment, then it is more likely that time will be saved earlier on in the implementation process. If a department or whole institution is investing in and supporting the use of CAA, economies of scale will help to ensure that more substantial timesavings are made.

Using CAA can demand a cultural shift in terms of the distribution of time invested in assessing student learning. Academics need to invest time prior to the event, rather than after it. This may be a difficult adjustment to make, particularly if it leads to clashes with other busy times in the academic year. Timesavings for academic staff may be as a result of a redistribution of workload from academic to administrative and technical support staff. This may be a valuable approach but needs to be planned and acknowledged. Timesavings resulting from a decrease in marking load must be offset against time required for assessment design and operational procedures. Medium- to long-term savings may be more achievable than immediate short-term gains.

Administrative efficiency

CAA provides assessment marks in electronic format and, therefore, the potential exists to make the administration and management of assessment data more efficient by automatically entering marks into student record systems and management information systems. The approach can save time and effort and reduce clerical errors. It does require systems to be compatible with CAA software or for an appropriate interface to be created between two or more systems. Other administrative efficiency gains may be made in terms of the collation of marks for examination boards, the reduction in the number of examination papers which require printing and the administration of collecting, logging and distributing assignments and examination papers to academic staff.

Advantages and disadvantages of CAA

There are many potential advantages to using CAA, which can be summarised as follows:

- Lecturers can monitor the progress of students through more frequent assessments.
- Students can monitor their own progress; self-assessment can be promoted.
- Detailed, specific feedback is available to students during and immediately after testing.
- Students acquire IT skills.
- More frequent assessment of students is made possible by the automatic marking of scripts.
- Large groups are more easily assessed, quickly and consistently.
- Potential to introduce graphics and multimedia allows for inclusion of questions not possible with paper assessments.
- Quality of questions can be easily monitored by statistical analysis.
- Diagnostic reports and analyses can be generated.
- Aids the transmission and administration of marks that can be automatically entered into information management systems and student records databases.
- Eliminates the need for double marking.
- Marking is not prone to human error.
- Assessments can be made available 'on demand' to support flexible learning.
- Adaptive testing can be used to match the test to the student's ability.
- Students can be provided with clues and marked accordingly.
- Randomisation of questions, which reduces the potential for cheating.
- Potential for sharing questions via question banks.

CAA also has its disadvantages. Some of the limitations are:

- Initial implementation of a CAA system can be costly and time-consuming.
- Hardware and software must be carefully monitored to avoid failure during examinations.
- Students must acquire adequate IT skills and experience of the assessment type in advance of the examination.
- Assessors and invigilators need training in assessment design, IT skills and examinations management.
- High level of coordination is required of all parties involved in assessment (academics, support staff, computer services, administrators).
- Question types supported by CAA systems are limited.

This chapter has offered a brief definition of and introduction to CAA, and many of the issues raised above are discussed in greater length in the rest of the book. In particular, Chapter 2 takes a more critical view of CAA and positions its development and use within broader contexts such as recent thinking on formative and summative assessment, learning technologies, and assessment, control and empowerment.

Chapter 2

Contexts for CAA

The combination of assessment and technology means that CAA potentially touches many aspects of learning and teaching in higher education, including the value of peer and self-assessment, suitability of question and examination types in different disciplines, the role of online learning, and issues of power within the examining process. This chapter will attempt to locate CAA within current thinking about assessment and online learning. In particular, it will consider recent research on summative and formative assessment; student participation in the assessment process; the significance of electronic literacy; and issues of control in the context of CAA.

Introduction

The use of CAA is influenced by (and, to some extent, has an impact upon) current issues within the arena of assessment, such as warrants and claims educators make on the basis of assessment (Knight, 2002b); the growth in participative assessment activities, in which students share with lecturers the process of making judgements about their work (Reynolds and Trehan, 2000; Brew, 1999; Boud, 1995); and the effect of assessment upon student learning. Particular issues that arise in relation to CAA include the frequency with which students are assessed, the appropriateness of certain question formats (eg multiple-choice), the role and nature of feedback, the participation by students in their assessment and potential loss of control within automated testing processes. Virtually all of these topics are relevant to other assessment methods (exams, essays, portfolios etc), but the introduction of computers into assessment intensifies the gaze into certain practices.

CAA is also positioned within the expanding range of learning technologies and therefore is pertinent to debates on the growth of online education, such as the development of virtual learning environments, students' relationships with technology, and issues of access and empowerment. Moreover, with the integration of CAA with other computerised systems, technical standards and security come into play, all of which remove certain elements of the assessment process from the context of the discipline and the academics responsible for the content. (However, it should be pointed out that there are a number of aspects of this process that are beyond the control of subject specialists even with traditional assessment.)

Additionally, CAA can find itself, unlike other assessment methods, operating at the interface between industry and education. There is, for example, a line of argument which suggests that software developers are at least influencing, if not determining, pedagogic practice by including certain question formats, enabling specific feedback processes, and embedding specific formulae for scoring. Furthermore, the cost of assessment software might determine which products are purchased by institutions, which in turn has an impact upon the type of test formats available.

Disciplinarity

Assessment is one of the ways in which students 'internalise' a discipline's standards and its notion of quality (Gibbs, 1999). Barnett (1995) argues that computer-based learning should be introduced into the curriculum, not as a transferable skill, but rather, where it enhances an understanding of the traditions of a discipline. Similarly, CAA, too, should be included when it can be tied directly to disciplinary knowledge and understanding. Significantly, in the past ten years, computer-based work (in the form of research, modelling, simulation, construction of corpuses etc) has come to feature in most disciplines. If computers have a role in teaching and learning, it seems appropriate that they should also be part of assessment practices. Indeed, in her overview of sector-wide assessment systems, according to subject review audits, Glasner (1999) reports that in English, departments were criticised for an over-reliance upon traditional written exams which neglected the assessment of stated objectives of skills relating to 'the use of IT'. A national survey into CAA conducted in 1999 found that while there was some use of CAA in nearly every subject area (as defined by the UK Higher Education Funding Council subject centre categories), the majority of reported assessments were in computing, sciences, engineering and maths. However, there were a considerable number of examples of CAA in social science and humanities courses (McKenna *et al.*, in press; McKenna, 2000). As technology develops, particularly in conjunction with subject specialists, it is likely that CAA will become increasingly differentiated (particularly in terms of question formats) according to disciplinary requirements.

Summative vs. formative

In recent years there has been a movement away from end-of-course examinations towards the increased use of formative and in-course assessment in order to both diversify assessment methods and to offer students feedback during their study. Nonetheless, summative final examinations are still a widely-used means of assessing students.

Recently, the use of summative assessment and the claims being made about student achievement on the strength of summative examinations have been challenged by Knight, who asserts that summative practices are in 'disarray' (Knight, 2002b). He argues that summative assessment is problematic in part because although it is held to account for the complex learning outcomes that higher education (HE) claims to provide, whether current assessments actually measure what they claim to is debatable. Furthermore, he suggests that the quest for reliability 'tends to skew assessment towards the assessment of simple and unambiguous achievements', while cost considerations may also tend to undermine the assessment of complex learning, which is an expensive task to undertake (Knight, 2002b). He suggests that because 'high stakes' assessment measures – those grades which appear on transcripts and lead to awards – must be seen to be 'robust' (in legal and other ways), they often fall back on those things which are believed to be assessed reliably. This means that what can be judged reliably (and often easily) is what gets attention from students and academics and that activities and understandings which fall outside such summative assessment are neither 'recorded nor celebrated' (Knight, 2002b).

The use of CAA for formative assessment may go some way towards resolving 'curriculum skew' and the lack of acknowledgement for formative work. One of the potential advantages of CAA is that it enables the collection of detailed data on formative activities. (This must be balanced against the surveillance concerns highlighted by Land and Bayne (2002).) In this sense, perhaps, CAA offers a sort of bridge between formative and summative assessments. Although Knight sees the two as distinct, others including Brown (1999) suggest that the line between formative and summative is a blurred one which is more to do with when the assessments are delivered and what is done with the marking and feedback rather than a precise difference in kind. With CAA, a useful term coined by Mackenzie (1999) is 'scored formative', which describes computerised coursework for which numerical scores are automatically assigned and recorded.

Student participation in assessment

The role of students within the assessment process is being given increased prominence (Reynolds and Trehan, 2000; Boud, 1995; Orsmond et al., 1997). Peer and self-assessment have become increasingly popular in higher education in recent years, particularly in medical education, where the capacity to judge one's own performance is seen as highly important (Antonelli, 1997; Evans et al., 2002). Self-assessment (like CAA) describes an approach, or, as Brown et al. (1997) suggest, a 'source', rather than a method. Thus there are a number of ways in which standard assessment practices can be adapted to enable students to assess themselves. In terms of CAA, formats such as MCQs, simulations and programmes which prompt a step-by-step reflection upon written work could all be used for self-assessment purposes.

A number of reasons for using self-assessment techniques have been identified by Brown et al. (1997), building upon Boud (1995). These include the opportunity for self-monitoring, diagnosis and remediation, and the consolidation of learning. Brew (1999) observes that trends towards involving students in their own assessment are indicative of more 'holistic' conceptions of learning and the role of assessment within it. Assessment is increasingly not just 'done' to students, but rather something in which they participate and have some element of ownership.

Boud (1995) suggests that self-assessment consists of two main parts: the development of criteria and the application of criteria to the task being evaluated. In the most common use of CAA, in which students' answers to objective questions are automatically scored, the student is not usually participating in the construction of criteria. In fact, much CAA activity would constitute what Brew (1999) calls 'self-testing', in which a student compares his/her responses to predetermined answers and feedback.

However, it is possible in a computerised system for students to generate questions, scoring options and feedback, thus participating, to some degree, in the creation of criteria. Indeed, if computer-based question templates are used, then the online publishing of questions and feedback by students for others to use is quite straightforward. Furthermore, one of the opportunities available within CAA question banks is the capacity for a student to select and build self-assessment exercises according to criteria such as topic, difficulty and question format. One of the advantages with automated marking and feedback is that students can compare their responses with a set of standards, receive feedback (albeit predetermined) and still preserve the anonymity of self-assessment. Moreover, Brew (1999) observes that the ability to self-assess is one that must be developed over time with practice. CAA self-assessment could be seen as part of the early stages of developing the capacity to judge and reflect upon one's own work. Thus a CAA self-test may function as the first step within a larger act of self-assessment. That is, a student may choose to perform a self-test on a particular topic, determine that s/he wishes to study further certain aspects based upon performance, and then reflect on other ways in which knowledge in these areas might be constructed and extended. The CAA test would act as a catalyst to further reflection on a theme.

In terms of peer assessment, online education would seem to be engendering new approaches to collaborative learning and assessment. Robinson (1999) writes of using computers for large-scale, anonymous peer reviewing exercises that would be unfeasible outside of a networked environment. Morgan and O'Reilly (1999) describe a number of case studies in which computer conferencing enables innovative, peer assessment activities involving the construction and evaluation of websites, organisation and contribution to online symposia, peer review, asynchronous discussions and debates, and group problem-solving. They argue that in computerised learning environments, distance learners, in particular, increasingly expect to participate in developing assessment tasks and criteria and in negotiating their marks and those of others. CAA and online learning will be considered further in Chapter 8.

Electronic literacy and CAA

As computerised assessments move beyond the simple transference of tests from paper to screen (what Bennett (1998) has termed first generation tests) to more sophisticated assessments which exploit the full range of options attendant upon online delivery (such as sound, image, hypertext etc), then issues of electronic literacy become significant. Such CAA requires students to be conversant with multimedia, simulations, online screen design, interpretation of audio and video clips etc. Thus CAA becomes more than the assessment of subject expertise, it also involves an understanding of how online environments mediate and even construct information and knowledge.

Electronic literacy encompasses an understanding of how to locate, organise and make use of digital information along with an awareness of the intricacies of online communication, knowledge creation and research (Shetzer and Warschauer, 2000). Chief among the characteristics of electronic literacy is the capacity to interpret multimedia, particularly an ability to analyse and understand visual representations of knowledge. Digital environments are reviving visual modes of communication (Kress, 1998, Warschauer, 1999) and Kress (1998) argues that visual literacy will soon rival text-based discourse as the primary means of communication. Significantly, visual communication calls for different approaches to interpretation; whereas written language tends to rely upon a sequential narrative for its meaning, visual communication relies upon 'the logic of simultaneous presence of a number of elements and their spatial relation to each other' (Kress, 1998).

Images (still and moving) are undoubtedly features of future CAA. For example, arguing that broadcasts are historical artefacts in much the same way as newspaper articles, cartoons, letters, diaries etc, Bennett (1998) describes the incorporation of film clips in a CAA history examination in order to extend the range of source material on which students are assessed: 'The importance of electronic media in communicating information is clearly growing … perhaps we should evaluate not only how effectively people handle print but how well they reason with information from film, radio, TV, and computers' (Bennett, 1998).

Even in largely text-based CAA assignments and examinations, the shift towards the visual is apparent. For example, largely monochromic paper tests have given way to multicoloured screen displays, and written instructions (such as 'Please turn over') are replaced with icons representing such navigational actions (for example, arrows indicating forward and back). It would seem that, as CAA increasingly comes to rely upon the visual, developing the ability of students to work with images will be crucial.

But all this is not to say that text is not the main feature in online assessment. Far from it. And if, as Morgan and O'Reilly (1999) suggest, assessments involve peer review, website design and evaluation, and communication within online communities, then an understanding of discourse within hypertext and multi-voiced environments becomes important. In digital environments, acts of reading take on new meaning as students potentially become 'reader-authors' who construct their own pathways through material and potentially add text and links to a wider network of information (Snyder, 1998; Pincas, 2000). Not surprisingly, this shift in textuality demands new reading and interpretive practices. Burbules (1998) argues that current trends in electronic environments fail to encourage a sufficiently critical approach to reading hypertext, and he takes as his example a lack of understanding of the rhetorical function of hypertext links, which although often seen as simply neutral, functional devices, are potentially enacting relationships (between objects, text, images) which may be laden with value-judgements. A function of electronic literacy would be therefore to explore critical approaches to the reading or interpretation of hypertext in much the same way that students might be taught to think about literature, history, visual art etc. Currently, educators are geared to evaluate written and sometimes spoken answers. With emergent forms of learning and assessment, it will become important to integrate teaching of electronic literacy into the curriculum and to develop techniques for assessing image- and sound-based responses; non-linear, hypertext discourse and jointly constructed work.

Issues of control

Issues of control, authority and autonomy for staff and students are increasingly part of the discourse of higher education, particularly in the contexts of assessment, student-centred learning and the integration of communication and information technology in the curriculum (Knight, 2002a; Land and Bayne, 2002; Brew, 1999). All three areas potentially converge within the practice of CAA, and it is possible to raise questions about control and empowerment with respect to CAA from the perspectives of students, academics and educationalists.

As the chief determinant of degree classification and thus students' success, assessment is arguably the most critical activity in which students take part in higher education, yet often the one over which they have least control. Reynolds and Trehan (2000) assert that examining also reinforces institutional power: 'assessment embodies power relations between the institution and its students, with tutors as custodians of the institution's rules and practices.' Creme (1995) argues that summative examination represents 'the most extreme form of teacher control' in which the entire process including content, timing and the environment is dictated by academics. Similarly, Boud (1995) suggests that lecturers assess 'too much and too powerfully' without sufficient consideration of the manner in which students experience such power enacted upon them.

With the emergence of a post-Dearing learning and teaching agenda in UK HE, assessment practices and their impact on student learning have come under increased scrutiny. As new, flexible approaches to learning such as self-directed, resource-based and distance learning are embraced, assessment, particularly CAA, is potentially an area where the locus of control is shifting towards students (Brew, 1999). At the same time, the nature of the academic identity is changing (Henkel, 2000), and it is perceived that traditional areas of authority and responsibility of lecturers are being challenged. Holley and Oliver (2000) argue that increased managerial 'involvement' in issues of pedagogy and curriculum design, coupled with moves towards student-centred approaches to learning, have empowered managers and students at the expense of academics. They also consider the introduction of learning technologies into teaching and suggest that here, too, control of the lecturer (in areas such as presentation, design, learning method, and sometimes even content) can be eroded. While they do not address CAA directly, the topics are closely related, and their framework for mapping and analysing the possible shifts in authority of different groups within higher education may be relevant to CAA.

Finally, work in the area of virtual and managed learning environments is now at the forefront of such research into educational technologies. One person's notion of electronic management and transference of electronic data is potentially another person's notion of control and surveillance, and the latter is beginning to be explored by Land and Bayne (2002) in terms of Foucauldian power constructs.

Academics and CAA

In the case of CAA, issues of control can be considered from the perspective of a range of individuals involved (staff, students, learning technologists, educationalists etc) in terms of the assessment process as well as assessment content. Academics, as suggested above, may find that responsibility in the assessment process is now shared with learning technologists and staff from computer services, who might determine, in part, issues of presentation, design and delivery. Similarly, because the use of CAA often requires new and restricted question formats, academics may share the writing process with educationalists. Additionally, institution-wide regulations and quality assurance procedures, which are often advocated in CAA literature (Stephens et al., 1998; McKenna and Bull, 2000; King, 1997) may impose certain constraints upon the examining process. Thus, while some find the use of automated marking liberating, it is possible that others may feel they have lost ownership of aspects of the assessment process.

Students and CAA

Potential issues of control from the student perspective can again be framed in terms of process and content. Lecturers tend to report that students are positive about the practice of CAA, (see Chapter 11) and

Holley and Oliver (2000) suggest that learning technologies can act as agents of empowerment for students. However, an issue that could usefully be considered in this context is the perceived rigidity of marking procedures (Bull *et al.*, in press). In particular, students have expressed the view that there are reduced opportunities for markers to exercise judgement when partially correct or contested answers are returned. This is largely a function of objective test questions, and the lack of opportunities for students to express themselves in objective formats is an area of control that has been considered elsewhere. For example, Paxton (2000) argues that multiple-choice questioning can be disempowering, because all the authority (in terms of meaning, ideas, knowledge etc) lies with the question writer and no voice is given to the student, who is a passive participant in the activity: 'The multiple-choice format … reinforces the idea that someone else already knows the answer to the question so original reinterpretations are not expected.' Arguably, CAA can make it harder for students to challenge aspects of the question material, the design and the process itself. By its very nature, the CAA process is perhaps more prescriptive than other, more negotiated, assessment activities, such as posters, presentations, portfolios etc. On the other hand, students who are using CAA for self-assessment and formative reasons may feel that they are better able to control the environment, timing and location of assessment with CAA as well as the frequency with which they access tests. Furthermore, as CAA methods develop, moving beyond objective testing and becoming more interactive, it may be that students are freer to express understanding in ways that are not available in traditional assessment formats, such as constructing knowledge using computer graphics, simulation, film, online dialogue etc.

Chapter 3

Objective tests

This chapter defines objective testing and considers how it is used in higher education. Pedagogical issues are addressed, and the assessment of a range of learning levels with objective test questions is discussed.

What are objective tests?

Objective tests require a user to choose or provide a response to a question whose correct answer is predetermined. Such a question might require a student to:

- select a solution from a set of choices;
- identify an object or position;
- supply brief numeric or text responses;
- input a mathematical expression for evaluation.

The question (or stem) is usually followed by the correct response (key) and a number of incorrect responses (distracters). Because the correct answers to objective test questions are predetermined, this type of assessment is well-suited to the many forms of CAA that involve automated marking. The electronic marking of the responses is non-subjective because no judgement has to be made on the correctness or otherwise of an answer at the time of marking. However, it is worth remembering that in terms of in-built bias, an objective test is only as objective as the test's designer makes it. For a list of different question types, see Chapter 4.

Background

Recent rises in student numbers have led to a re-evaluation of the type and frequency of assessments. Marking large numbers of student essays, projects and other subjective assessments is time-consuming, labour-intensive and prone to errors of consistency (Newstead and Dennis, 1994). Including objective tests within an assessment profile can allow more regular and faster examining of students, particularly if automated marking is used. Additionally, CAA may eliminate the need for double (and triple) marking, thus saving time after the examination process. Objective tests also enable the assessment of a wide range of topics within a single test.

Objective testing is probably more widespread than most people realise. In the United States (US), for example, large-scale national objective tests, such as the American College Testing examination, the Scholastic Aptitude Tests, the Graduate Record Examinations and the Law Society Admissions Test are used as performance indicators for all students seeking admission to undergraduate and postgraduate courses. These tests are regarded as the sector standard and have been in operation, in some cases, for over 40 years. They are increasingly delivered via computer networks in invigilated test centres across the country. (For more information, see the Education Testing Service website, http://www.ets.org, accessed 4 January 2003.) Objective tests are also widely used in Australia, Singapore and South Africa.

In the United Kingdom (UK), the use of objective testing for formative and summative examinations is increasingly popular. A recent survey into the use of CAA in UK higher education (HE) found that over 80 universities and colleges of higher education reported some use of CAA, most of which involves objective tests. Of these, there were 42 pre-1992 universities and 32 post-1992 universities. According to the survey, CAA is predominantly used in computing, sciences and mathematics; however, there is evidence of some use in social sciences and humanities courses (Bull and McKenna, 2000).

Pedagogical issues

Objective tests are especially well-suited to certain types of tasks. Because questions can be designed to be answered quickly, they allow lecturers to test students on a wide range of material. The use of CAA in the delivery of objective tests enables the provision of automatic feedback (in terms of scores, hints, praise and guidance) to the student. Additionally, statistical analysis on the performance of individual students, cohorts and questions is possible.

The capacity of objective tests to assess a wide range of learning is often underestimated. Objective tests are good at examining recall of facts, knowledge and application of terms, and questions that require short text, numerical or mathematical expression responses. But a common worry is that objective tests cannot assess learning beyond basic comprehension.

However, questions that are constructed imaginatively can challenge students and test higher learning levels. For example, students can be presented with case studies or a collection of data (such as a set of medical symptoms) and be asked to provide an analysis by answering a series of questions. If using a computer, students can be given electronic tools to manipulate or construct objects on a screen. Problem solving can also be assessed with the right type of questions. Assessing higher learning levels with objective test questions will be considered more closely below.

Concern is sometimes expressed that some objective tests, notably multiple-choice questions, result in inflated scores due to guessing. However, the effects of guessing can be eliminated through a combination of question design and scoring techniques. With the right number of questions and distracters, distortion through guessing becomes largely irrelevant. Alternatively, guessing can be encouraged and measured if this is thought to be a desirable skill. (See Chapter 6 for a fuller discussion of scoring issues, including negative marking and confidence assessment.)

There are, however, limits to what objective tests can assess. They cannot, for example, test a student's ability to communicate, to construct arguments or to offer original responses. Tests must be carefully constructed in order to avoid the de-contextualisation of knowledge (Paxton, 2000) and it is wise to use objective testing as only one of a variety of assessment methods within a module. However, in times of growing student numbers and decreasing resources, objective testing can offer a valuable and viable addition to the range of assessment types available to a lecturer. Table 3.1 provides a summary of some of the advantages and disadvantages of objective tests.

Tests

Objective tests fit within the definitions for assessment types given in the Introduction. There are a number of ways in which objective tests can be used.

- *Diagnostic* Such tests may help a lecturer modify course content to fit students' needs or identify students who need additional help or do not need to take modules.
- *Self-assessment* If mounted on a computer network, it is easier for tests to be taken repeatedly and students can learn from their mistakes by using the feedback provided. Additionally, the process is non-threatening and self-paced.
- *Formative assessment* Lecturers may wish to use objective tests at regular intervals within a course to determine which topics have been understood and to motivate students to keep pace with the teaching of

Table 3.1 Advantages and disadvantages of objective testing

The *advantages* of objective testing can include:
- Significantly reduced marking time (especially using CAA).
- Speed of assessment (a large number of questions can be asked quickly).
- Wider coverage of topic content than essay questions; scope of test is broadened.
- Analysis of individual questions.
- Provision of automatic feedback to student (when used in CBA; automatic feedback not possible with OMR).
- Potential for more frequent assessment.
- Questions can be pre-tested in order to evaluate their effectiveness and level of difficulty.

The *disadvantages* of objective testing can include:
- Significant amount of time required to construct good questions.
- Writing questions that test higher order skills requires much effort.
- Cannot assess written expression or creativity.

the module. In order to encourage students to treat such formative assessments seriously, a course requirement might be set which stipulates that in order to pass the module, a minimum score (40 per cent, for example) would have to be obtained on all tests. Similarly, such tests could be used to encourage lecture attendance and regular learning.

- *Summative*   Objective tests can be used to test the range of the student's understanding of course material. As above, it has been suggested that the capacity of objective tests to examine the breadth of a topic or module can be used to motivate good attendance, because lecturers can assess a wider range of material in one examination (Kniveton, 1996).

What types of learning can be tested using objective tests?

Bloom's taxonomy of educational objectives (Bloom *et al.*, 1956) is a useful starting point for categorising types of questions (see Table 3.2).

It is commonly assumed that objective tests are only useful for examining the first three or four levels of learning defined by Bloom *et al.* (1956). However, some educationalists, including McBeath (1992), suggest

Table 3.2   Bloom's Taxonomy and Question categories

Competence	Skills demonstrated
Knowledge	Recall of information Knowledge of facts, dates, events, places Question words: list, define, label, describe, name
Comprehension	Interpretation of information in one's own words Grasping meaning Question words: interpret, discuss, predict, summarise, classify
Application	Application of methods, theories, concepts to new situations Question words: apply, demonstrate, show, relate
Analysis	Identification of patterns Recognition of components and their relationships Question words: analyse, arrange, order, explain, connect, infer, compare, categorise
Synthesis	Generalise from given knowledge Use old ideas to create new ones Organise and relate knowledge from several areas Draw conclusions, predict Question words: integrate, modify, invent, design, compose, plan, formulate, arrange
Evaluation	Make judgements Assess value of ideas, theories Compare and discriminate between ideas Evaluate data Question words: appraise, judge, evaluate, defend, rank, conclude, discriminate, recommend

Source: Table based on the work of Bloom *et al.* (1956).

that all six levels can be tested using objective test questions. The questions on the following pages exemplify the different levels of Bloom's taxonomy.

Level 1   Knowledge

Aim To recall a specific date
Question In which year did the American Civil War end?

    a   1832
    b   1857

c   1865*
d   1888

Level 2   Comprehension

Aim To understand and interpret definitions, relationships and analogies
Question In the following, a related pair of words is followed by four more pairs of words. Choose the response pair that best expresses a relationship similar to that expressed in the original pair.

QUENCH : THIRST

a   staunch : wound
b   douse : fever
c   antidote : poison
d   extinguish : fire*

Level 3   Application

Aim To calculate velocity
Question End A of the cord is moving 6 m/s to the left. Compute the velocity of the block B and select one of the responses below.

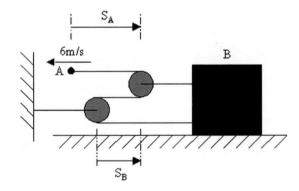

Figure 3.1

Note
Question created by Rob Kay and Fiona Lamb at Loughborough University, Faculty of Engineering. For a full range of their self-assessment MCQs in engineering, see the following site: http://www.lboro.ac.uk/faculty/eng/engtlsc/Eng_Mech/tutorials/tut12_8.txt (accessed January 2003).

a   2 m/s (to left)
b   3 m/s (to left)*
c   6 m/s (to left)
d   12 m/s (to left)
e   none of the above

Level 4   Analysis

Aim To analyse and infer from a geological map

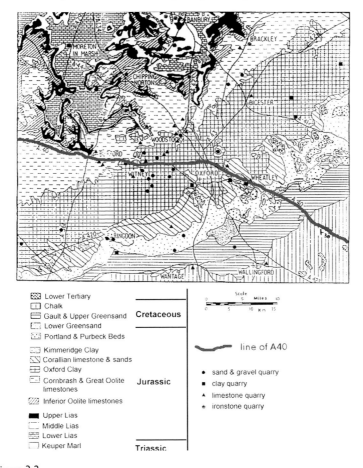

Lower Tertiary
Chalk
Gault & Upper Greensand   **Cretaceous**
Lower Greensand
Portland & Purbeck Beds

Kimmeridge Clay
Corallian limestone & sands
Oxford Clay
Cornbrash & Great Oolite   **Jurassic**
limestones
Inferior Oolite limestones

Upper Lias
Middle Lias
Lower Lias
Keuper Marl   **Triassic**

Scale
Miles
Km

~~~ line of A40

● sand & gravel quarry
■ clay quarry
▲ limestone quarry
✳ ironstone quarry

Figure 3.2

Note
This exercise and the following questions are part of a larger assessment created by Dr
Roger Suthren at Oxford Brookes University. The full assessment is located at:
http://www.brookes.ac.uk/geology/8307/a40frame.html (accessed January 2003).

Study the geological sketch map of Oxfordshire (on p. 25) which shows the trace of the A40 road route, and read the notes on the geological problems encountered by engineers in building roads (linear route). For the purpose of this exercise assume that the whole of this A40 route is going to be upgraded to motorway standards involving major reconstruction (in reality there is no current proposal to do this!).

Question 1   Landslips
At which of the following contacts between strata would you expect most landslips to occur? Choose two of the following options.

    a   Chalk above Gault Clay
    b   Gault Clay above Lower Greensand
    c   Corallian limestone above Oxford Clay
    d   Cornbrash limestone above
    e   Inferior Oolite limestone

Question 2   Swelling and shrinkage
Which of the following rock units are most likely to show shrinkage and swelling with fluctuating dry and wet periods? Choose two of the following options:

    a   Chalk
    b   Gault Clay
    c   Lower Greensand
    d   Kimmeridge Clay
    e   Inferior Oolite limestone

Level 5   Synthesis

Aim To organise and arrange appropriate critical terms in order to construct a geological analysis of the following photographic image of a rock formation.

Question Move the appropriate descriptive terms from the list to the 'form' and 'attitude' boxes below.

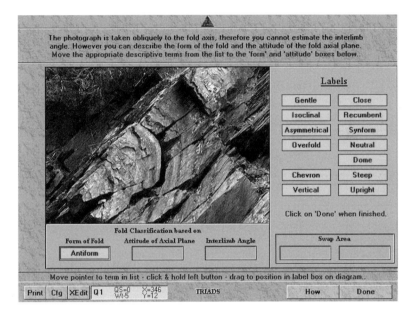

Figure 3.3

Note
Question created by Professor Don Mackenzie, TRIADS. For a full demonstration of TRIADS, see http://www.derby.ac.uk/assess/talk/quicdemo.html (accessed January 2003).

Level 6: Evaluation

Aim   To assess the condition of a patient based on various readings

---

Question: An adult subject breathing air was found to have the
following lung volumes:
  • Vital capacity – 3.5 litres
  • Forced expiratory volume in 1 sec (FEV1) – 2.8 litres
  • Functional residual capacity (FRC) – 1.8 litres
  • Residual volume (RV) – 0.8 litre

True   False
☐   ☐   a There is no obstruction to airflow. (T)
☐   ☐   b The subject must be abnormal. (F)
☐   ☐   c The expiratory reserve volume is 1 litre. (T)
☐   ☐   d All of these measurements could have been made using
                  only a spirometer. (F)
☐   ☐   e There would be approximately 250 ml of oxygen in this
                  subject's lungs at the end of a tidal expiration. (T)

Figure 3.4

Note
Question created by Dr David A. Davies, The University of Birmingham, MEDWEB
Computer-assisted Assessment website: http://medweb.bham.ac.uk/caa (accessed January
2003).

The extent to which questions test different levels of learning will depend
on the subject, context and level of the course or module. For example, a
question which seeks to test the analytical skills of first year undergraduates may test only knowledge and comprehension in third year students.
There are also different interpretations of the terms 'analysis', 'synthesis'
and 'evaluation'. Bloom's taxonomy can serve as a useful framework but
may need to be refined to meet the needs of a specific assessment or course.

Objective tests can test across a wide range of knowledge and abilities;
however, designing questions to test higher order skills can be time-
consuming and requires skill and creativity (Haladyna, 1997). It is important to determine where and how objective tests can be used most produc-
tively and effectively within a given course/module. Chapter 7 provides a
more detailed account of constructing tests and integrating them with
existing assessment methods.

Chapter 4

Writing questions

This chapter looks closely at different question formats suitable for CAA using objective tests and offers detailed suggestions for constructing effective test items. The chapter discusses different types of questions and explores how these can be used to test various levels of learning. McBeath (1992) and Heard et al. (1997b) offer similar approaches and Haladyna (1997) offers practical examples of writing questions to test higher levels of learning.

Question types

The following are examples of some of the question types appropriate for CAA:

- Multiple-choice questions (MCQs) are the traditional 'choose one from a list' of possible answers.
- True/false questions require a student to assess whether a statement is true or not.
- Assertion/reason questions combine elements of MCQ and true/false.
- Multiple-response questions (MRQs) are similar to MCQs, but involve the selection of more than one answer from a list.
- Graphical hotspot questions involve selecting an area(s) of the screen, by moving a marker to the required position. Advanced types of hotspot questions include labelling and building questions.
- Text/numerical questions involve the input of text or numbers at the keyboard. These are often known as text match, gap-fill or fill-in-the-blank. The checking process for such answer types generally relies on string recognition techniques.
- Matching questions involves linking items in one list to items in a second list.

- Sore finger questions have been used in language teaching and computer programming, where one word, code or phrase is out of keeping with the rest of a passage. It could be presented as a hotspot or text input type of question.
- Ranking questions require the student to relate items in one column to another and can be used to test the knowledge of sequences, order of events, level of gradation.
- Sequencing questions require the student to position text or graphic objects in a given sequence. These are particularly good for testing methodology.
- Field simulation questions offer simulations of real problems or exercises.

Other question types require students to identify and/or manipulate images. Students may be asked to plot a graph, complete a matrix, draw a line or build up an image using parts provided.

Constructing multiple-choice questions

Parts of a multiple-choice question

A traditional MCQ (or item) is one in which a student chooses one answer from a number of choices supplied. An MCQ consists of four discrete elements (see Figure 4.1):

- *stem*   the text of the question
- *options*   the choices provided after the stem
- *key*   the correct answer in the list of options
- *distracters*   the incorrect answers in the list of options

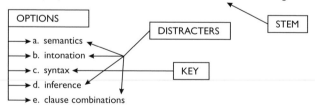

As children's language skills increase in complexity, from the pre-linguistic phase to telegraphic speech, the progression is most noticeable in which one of the following areas?

OPTIONS

DISTRACTERS

STEM

→ a. semantics
→ b. intonation
→ c. syntax
→ d. inference
→ e. clause combinations

KEY

Figure 4.1 Parts of a multiple-choice question

The following sections provide good practice guidelines for writing questions and distracters.

Writing stems

1 Present a single, definite statement to be completed or answered by one of the several given choices.

    A Weak question – Morphemes:

    a are made up of smaller units called phenomes
    b are NOT found in grammatical function words
    c create meaning or have a grammatical function
    d can be described as free or bound

    B Improved question – Morphemes are the smallest contrastive unit of:

    a compound words
    b prefixes
    c grammar
    d intransitive verbs

In Example A, there is no sense from the stem what the question is asking. The second example more clearly identifies the question and offers the student a set of homogeneous choices.

2 Avoid unnecessary and irrelevant material.

    A Weak question – Paul Muldoon, an Irish post-modern poet who uses experimental and playful language, uses which poetic genre in 'Why Brownlee Left'?

    a sonnet
    b elegy
    c narrative poem
    d dramatic monologue
    e haiku

    B Improved question – Paul Muldoon uses which poetic genre in 'Why Brownlee Left'?

    a sonnet
    b elegy
    c narrative poem

    d   dramatic monologue
    e   haiku

3   Use clear, straightforward language in the stem of the item. Questions that are constructed using complex wording may become a test of reading comprehension rather than an assessment of whether the student knows the subject matter.

    A   *Weak question* – In order to optimise the inherent shielding of polymers from radio frequency interference and electromagnetic sources, it is customarily the case that conductive fillers are utilised, but the possible benefit of employing metal vapour deposition as a potential substitute might be:

    a   Metal vapour deposition is less complex while simultaneously enhancing overall
    b   The conductive properties of the polymer surface are enhanced energy efficiency factors
    c   The cost factor is diminished
    d   The mechanical properties of metal filled polymers are often non-optimal
    e   Both b and d

    B   *Improved question* – Radio Frequency Interference (RFI) and Electro Magnetic Interference (EMI) shielding of polymers can be provided by conductive fillers. Why might metal vapour deposition be used instead?

    a   Metal vapour deposition is simpler and more energy efficient
    b   It gives the polymer a better conductive surface
    c   It costs less
    d   Mechanical properties of metal filled polymers often suffer
    e   Both b and d

4   Use negatives sparingly. If negatives must be used, capitalise, underscore, embolden or otherwise highlight.

    A   *Weak question* – Which of the following is not a symptom of osteoporosis?

    a   decreased bone density
    b   frequent bone fractures
    c   raised body temperature
    d   lower back pain

B   *Improved question* – Which of the following is a symptom of osteoporosis?

a   decreased bone density
b   raised body temperature
c   hair loss
d   painful joints

5   Put as much of the question in the stem as possible, rather than duplicating material in each of the options (Gronlund, 1988).

A   *Weak question* – Maslow's theory of growth motivation asserts that:

a   humanistic needs are physiological
b   humanistic needs are emotional
c   humanistic needs are intellectual
d   humanistic needs are social

B   *Improved question* – Maslow's theory of growth motivation asserts that humanistic needs are:

a   physiological
b   emotional
c   intellectual
d   social

Writing distracters

1   For single-response MCQs, ensure that there is only one correct response.

A   *Weak question* – Which of the following texts is considered to represent the pinnacle of modernist achievement?

a   *The Waste Land*
b   *Middlemarch*
c   'Ode to a Nightingale'
d   *Ulysses*
e   *Ethan Frome*

B   *Improved question* – Which of the following texts represents one of the high points of modernist achievement?

a   *The Waste Land*

b   *Middlemarch*
c   'Ode to a Nightingale'
d   *Ethan Frome*
e   'My Last Duchess'

In Example A, both options 'a' and 'd' could be considered to be correct.

2   Use only plausible and attractive alternatives as distracters.

> A   *Weak question* – The Dichotic Listening Test determines which side of the brain is directly involved in:

a   depth perception
b   selection attention
c   cognition
d   hearing sounds

> B   *Improved question*: The Dichotic Listening Test determines which side of the brain is directly involved in:

a   tone perception
b   selection attention
c   pitch constancy
d   hearing sounds

In Example A, 'a' and 'c' are not plausible distracters.

3   Avoid giving clues to the correct answer.

> A   *Weak question* – A fertile area in the desert in which the water table reaches the ground surface is called an:

a   mirage
b   oasis
c   water hole
d   polder

> B   *Improved question* – A fertile area in the desert in which the water table reaches the ground surface is called a/an:

a   mirage
b   oasis
c   water hole
d   polder

Example A uses the article 'an' which identifies choice 'b' as the correct response. Ending the stem with 'a/an' improves the question.

4   If possible, avoid the choices 'all of the above' and 'none of the above'. It is tempting to resort to these alternatives but their use can be flawed. To begin with, they often appear as an alternative that is not the correct response. If you do use them, be sure that they constitute the correct answer part of the time. An 'all of the above' alternative could be exploited by test-wise students who will recognise it as the correct choice by identifying only two correct alternatives.

Similarly, a student who can identify one wrong alternative can then also rule this response out. Clearly, the students' chances of guessing the correct answer improve as they employ these techniques. Although a similar process of elimination is not possible with 'none of the above', it is the case that when this option is used as the correct answer, the question is only testing the students' ability to rule out wrong answers, and this does not guarantee that they know the correct one (Gronlund, 1988).

5   Distracters based on common student errors or misconceptions are very effective. One technique for compiling distracters is to ask students to respond to open-ended short-answer questions, perhaps as formative assessments. Identify which incorrect responses appear most frequently and use them as distracters for a multiple-choice version of the question.

6   Correct statements that do not answer the question are often strong distracters.

7   Avoid using ALWAYS and NEVER in the stem as students are likely to rule such universal statements out of consideration.

8   Use all options as keys equally.

9   Do not create distracters that are so close to the correct answer that they may confuse students who really know the answer to the question. 'Distracters should differ from the key in a substantial way, not just in some minor nuance of phrasing or emphasis' (Isaacs, 1994).

10   Provide a sufficient number of distracters.

You will probably choose to use three, four or five alternatives in a multiple-choice question. Until recently, it was thought that three or four distracters were necessary for the item to be suitably difficult. However, a

1987 study by Owen and Freeman suggests that three choices are sufficient (cited in Brown *et al.*, 1997). Clearly the higher the number of distracters, the less likely it is for the correct answer to be chosen through guessing (providing all alternatives are of equal difficulty).

Further examples of questions from a range of subject areas are given in Appendix A, including a set of weak and improved questions.

Other question types

Multiple-response questions

Multiple-response questions are a variation of multiple-choice questions in which the student is allowed to select more than one response. If desired, the test designer can withhold the number of correct responses from the student, thus making guessing the correct answer more difficult.

Which of the following are attributes of a virtual learning environment?

A It is based on a client-server architecture.

B It enables collaborative work between students.

C It requires participants to know HTML.

D It allows synchronous interaction between participants.

Figure 4.2 Multiple-response question

Matching

Matching items require students to match a series of stems or premises to a response or principle. They consist of a set of directions, a column of statements and a column of responses.

Matching questions are particularly good at assessing a student's understanding of relationships. They can test recall by requiring a student to match the following elements:

- definitions – terms
- historical events – dates
- achievements – people
- statements – postulates
- descriptions – principles (McBeath, 1992)

They can also assess a student's ability to apply knowledge by requiring the test-taker to match the following:

- examples – terms
- functions – parts
- classifications – structures
- applications – postulates
- problems – principles (McBeath, 1992)

Matching questions are really a variation of the multiple-choice format. If you find that you are writing MCQs which share the same answer choices, you may consider grouping the questions into a matching item. The following are tips for writing good matching questions:

- Provide clear directions.
- Keep the information in each column as homogeneous as possible.
- Allow the responses to be used more than once.
- Arrange the list of responses systematically if possible (chronological, alphabetical, numerical).
- Include more responses than stems to help prevent students using a process of elimination to answer the question.

Directions Column I contains descriptions of geographic characteristics of wind belts. For each statement find the appropriate wind belt in Column II. Record your answer in the appropriate space. Answers may be used more than once.

Column I	Column II
1 Region of high pressure, calm, and light winds	A Doldrums
2 The belt of calm air nearest the equator latitudes	B Horse
	C Polar easterlies
3 A wind belt in the northern hemisphere typified by a continual drying wind	D Prevailing easterlies
	E Prevailing westerlies
4 Most of the United States is found in this belt	

Figure 4.3 Matching test item

Source: Example from McBeath R. J. (Ed.) (1992), *Instructing and Evaluating Higher Education: A Guidebook for Planning Learning Outcomes,* New Jersey: ETP p. 207.

Directions Match the quotation in Column I with the literary school with which it is associated listed in Column II. Items in Column II may be used more than once.

Column I	Column II
1 You can lead a horse to water but you can't make it hold its nose to the grindstone and hunt with the hounds.	A Romanticism B Modernism C Neo-classicism
2 I cannot see what flowers are at my feet, Nor what soft incense hangs upon the boughs, But, in embalmed darkness, guess each sweet Wherewith the seasonable month endows The grass, the thicket, and the fruittree wild; White hawthorn, and the pastoral eglantine; Fast fading violets covered up in leaves; And mid-May's eldest child, The coming musk-rose, full of dewy wine, The murmurous haunt of flies on summer eves.	D Postmodernism E Humanism F Classical realism
3 frseeeeeeeefronnnng train somewhere whistling the strength those engines have in them like big giants and the water rolling all over and out of them all sides like the end of Loves old sweeeetsonnnng the poor men that have to be out all the night from their wives and families in those roasting engines stifling it was today Im glad I burned the half of those old Freemans and Photo Bits leaving things like that lying about hes getting very careless	
4 Twit twit twit Jug jug jug jug jug jug So rudely forc'd. Tereu	
5 A perfect Judge will read each Work of Wit With the same Spirit that its Author writ, Survey the Whole, nor seek slight Faults to find, Where Nature moves, and Rapture warms the Mind;	

Figure 4.4 Matching test item
Sources: (1) Paul Muldoon, 'Symposium', in *Hay*, Faber & Faber, 1998; (2) John Keats, 'Ode to a Nightingale', in *The Norton Anthology of Poetry*, W. W. Norton, 1970; (3) James Joyce, *Ulysses*, Penguin, 1990; (4) T. S. Eliot, 'The Waste Land', in *The Complete Poems and Plays*, Faber & Faber, 1969; (5) Alexander Pope, 'An Essay in Criticism', in *The Poems of Alexander Pope*, Routledge, 1963.

True/false questions

A true/false question is a specialised form of the multiple-choice format in which there are only two possible alternatives. These questions can be used when the test designer wishes to measure a student's ability to identify whether statements of fact are accurate or not.

> **T F** A poem with the following rhyme scheme could be correctly referred to as an English sonnet: abab cdcd efef gg.
>
> **T F** All eukaryotic genes are organised into operons.

Figure 4.5 True/false questions

True/false questions offer lecturers a very efficient method of testing a wide range of material in a short period of time. They can also be combined within an MCQ to create the more complex assertion-reason item. However, true/false questions do have a number of limitations:

- Guessing – a student has a one in two chance of guessing the correct answer to a question.
- It can be difficult to write a statement which is unambiguously true or false – particularly for complex material.
- The format does not discriminate among students of different abilities as well as other question types.

Suggestions for writing true/false questions:

- Include only one main idea in each item.
- As in MCQs generally, use negatives sparingly.
- Try using in combination with other material, such as graphs, maps, written material. This combination allows for the testing of more advanced learning outcomes (Gronlund, 1988).
- Use statements which are unequivocally true or false.
- Avoid lifting statements directly from assigned reading, lecture notes or other course materials so that recall alone will not permit a correct answer.
- Generally avoid the use of words which would signal the correct response to the test-wise student. Absolutes such as 'none', 'never', 'always', 'all', 'impossible' tend to be false, while qualifiers such as 'usually', 'generally', 'sometimes', 'often' are likely to be true.

Text match response

The text match question, also known as gap-fill or fill-in-the-blank, requires a student to supply an answer to a question or complete a blank within a brief piece of text, using words, symbols or numbers.

---

a A/an _____ is a plant which tolerates and flourishes on acid soils.

b $235 \times 23 + (9 \times 5) =$ _____

Figure 4.6 Text match questions

A possible advantage of this question type is that the student must supply the correct answer rather than identify or choose it. The likelihood that the candidate will guess the correct answer is lower than that of an MCQ. However, text match questions can be difficult to phrase in such a way that only a single correct answer is possible. Additionally, if you are marking the assessment with computers, spelling errors may disadvantage students who know the right answer. However, with some software, the test designer can identify numerous permutations of the correct answer for which the student will be awarded full marks. For example, if 'United States' were the correct response to a text match question, the author of the test could designate full marks to be awarded for all of the following: 'United States', 'US', 'USA' and 'United States of America'.

Example Find the complex number z where
$$z = (\{a\} + \{b\}i) (\{c\} + \{d\}i)$$
expressing the answer in the form x + yi with x and y real.

I $z = ? \{a * c - b * d\} + \{b * c + a * d\}i$

Figure 4.7 Mathematical question

Source: Question created by Professor Cliff Beevers, Heriot-Watt University.

Note
The use of the curly brackets $\{a\}$ etc indicates a random parameter which can take, for example, the values $-3, -2, -1, 1, 2, 3$ randomly and so would appear differently each time the question is run. The answer would also appear as numbers and not letters taking on the value indicated by $\{a * c - b * d\}$ etc. For checking purposes, answers with i can be treated as a function of variable I and the string evaluation technique again works well.

Mathematical expressions

As indicated in Chapter 3, it is possible to check for mathematical answers by using string evaluation techniques (see Beevers *et al.* (1991) and Beevers *et al.* (1992)). The example (in Figure 4.7) in multiplication of complex numbers also illustrates the role of randoms in mathematical computer-aided learning (CAL).

Graphical hotspot

A graphical hotspot question requires a student to identify a particular location on the screen, either by dragging and dropping a specified marker or by using keyboard arrow keys. This question format is used with graphics (such as maps, charts, representations of paintings, photographs and diagrams) and it is useful in subjects in which the interpretation of visual materials is required.

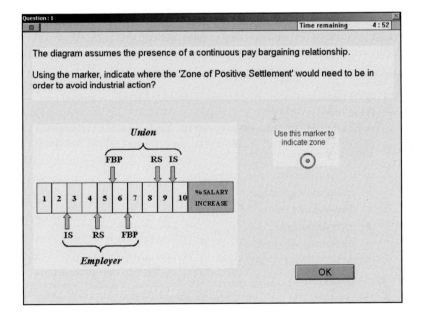

Figure 4.8 Graphical hotspot question

Advanced question types

Once you have tackled basic MCQs, you may wish to try more complicated forms such as multiple true/false and assertion-reason.

Multiple true/false questions

In a typical multiple true/false question, a student is presented with a scenario or set of data followed by three or more statements. The student must determine whether each statement is true or false. A series of true/false questions on a specific topic can test a deeper understanding of an issue. They can be structured to lead a student through a logical pathway (Brown *et al.*, 1997) such as a medical diagnosis or an analysis of a laboratory experiment (see Figure 4.9). Such questions may also be useful to the lecturer for diagnostic purposes, because by analysing students' responses, a tutor may be able to determine at what stage in the process misunderstandings are occurring. Additionally, in order to counter guessing, test designers may choose to award marks only for questions in which all parts have been answered correctly. Whereas a single true/false question carries a 50 per cent chance that a student will guess it correctly, a five-part multiple true/false question carries only a three per cent

---

I   *In the following question, the examiner is assessing whether the student can apply his/her knowledge:*

A 45-year-old asthmatic woman who has lived all her life in Glasgow presents with a goitre of four years' duration and clinical features suggestive of hypothyroidism. Likely diagnoses include

a   iodine deficiency

b   dyshormonogenesis

c   drug-induced goitre

d   thyroid cancer

e   auto-immune thyroiditis

(Correct answer: *true* C and E;   *false* A, B and D)

The student has to appreciate that in Great Britain iodine deficiency is not likely to be associated with hypothyroidism, that a 45-year-old patient with only a four-year history is unlikely to have dyshormonogenesis, that asthmatic patients not uncommonly take iodine-containing preparations which may result in a goitre, that hypothyroidism is not usually associated with thyroid cancer and that auto-immune thyroiditis typically is found in a middle-aged woman with hypothyroidism (from Brown *et al.*, 1997).

---

2   *In the following question, the student's clinical judgement is assessment*

A 28-year-old woman with one child has taken anti-thyroid drugs for 6 months for thyrotoxicosis. She has a friend who has been successfully treated with radio-iodine. She finds she frequently forgets to take her drugs and wants to stop them to have radio-iodine treatment.

a   She should be told that because of her age radio-iodine is best avoided.

b   The problems associated with radio-iodine should be discussed with her.

c   Surgery as a possible alternative should be discussed with her.

d   She should be advised that some form of further treatment is required.

e   You should find out more about her friend's treatment.

(Correct answer: *true* B, C and D;   *false* A and E).

Figure 4.9 Multiple true/false questions

Source: Examples from Harden, R.M. and Dunn, W.G. (1981), *Assessment Work Manual Dundee Centre of Medical Education* in Brown, *et al.* (1997).

chance that the student will arrive at the right answer solely through guessing.

The multiple true/false item is also better able to discriminate among students of different abilities than single true/false questions. However, as with standard true/false questions, it may be difficult to construct statements that are absolutely true or false.

Assertion/reason

The assertion/reason item combines elements of multiple-choice and true/false question types, and allows testing of more complicated issues and requires a higher level of learning.

The question consists of two statements, an assertion and a reason. The student must first determine whether each statement is true. If both are true, the student must next determine whether the reason correctly explains the assertion. Assertion/reason questions can be used to explore cause and effect and identify relationships. When writing assertion/reason questions, keep in mind the following points:

- The reason should be a free-standing sentence so that it can be considered separately from the assertion.
- Avoid using minor reasons. These can result in an ambiguous question.
- Repeat options A–E in full for each question.
- Use all five options as keys equally.

Each question below consists of an assertion and a reason. Indicate your answer from the alternatives below by circling the appropriate letter.

	Assertion	Reason
A	True	True – reason is correct explanation
B	True	True – reason is NOT correct explanation
C	True	False
D	False	True
E	False	False

Assertion

1 The blood sugar level falls rapidly after hepactectomy.
   BECAUSE
   The glycogen of the liver is the principal source of blood sugar.

2 Increased government spending increases inflation under all conditions.
   BECAUSE
   Government spending is not offset by any form of production.

3 Chloroform has a dipole moment.
   BECAUSE
   The chloroform molecule is tetrahedral.

Figure 4.10 Assertion/reason questions
Source: Quoted in Brown et al., 1997, p. 93 (based on Matthews, 1981).

Multi-stage mathematical question

Following the examples in Chapter 3 and earlier in this chapter, it is possible to set more complicated mathematical questions which require more than one answer. For example, Figure 4.11 describes a question with random parameters such that each time the question is presented, different numbers appear on screen.

Question:

Find the equation of the tangent to the curve defined parametrically by

$$x = \{a\}t^3 + \{b\}, \quad y = \{3c\}t^2 - \{d\}$$

at the point where t = 1. Write down a formula for dy/dx in terms of t and construct the equation of the tangent in the form y = mx + c at t = 1. Also, compute the value of d^2/dx^2 at the point t = −1.

1 dy/dx (in terms of t) is ? $\{2c\}/\{a\}t$

2 Equation of tangent at t = 1 is y = ? $\{2c\}x\{a\} + \{c - d - 2c^*b/a\}$

3 Value of d^2y/dx^2 at = −1 is ? $\{-2c/(3a^2)\}$

This question has been set with four random parameters and for ease of explanation let us suppose that a = 1,2,5; b = 2,4,7,8; c = 2,4,8; d = 1,3,5,7 so that each time this question is set, different numbers appear on the screen. Other combinations of the randoms are possible and in its latest incarnation the CALM assessment system, known as CUE, provides simplifications to reduce, for example, fractions to their neatest form. This question is typical of the questions set for Engineering and Science undergraduates in a course on parametric differentiation.

Figure 4.11 Multi-stage mathematical question

Source: Question provided by Professor Cliff Beevers, Heriot-Watt University

Note
CUE is currently an internal Heriot-Watt assessment system which has grown from a collaboration between the Computer-aided Learning in Mathematics (CALM) group, the University of Cambridge Local Examination Syndicate and the commercial company EQL International. Further details of CUE and CALM can be found at: http://www.scrolla.hw.ac.uk (accessed January 2003).

Case study question

A case study question is one which presents information in the form of a scenario or simulation which students must read and understand before responding to a series of questions. One advantage of the case study format is that it has the capacity to test higher level learning by requiring students to analyse material before answering questions.

Due to the amount of reading involved, case study questions generally take students longer to answer than more standard MCQs or T/F questions. Therefore, test designers should adjust time allowances for such assessments accordingly. Additionally, if the case study is lengthy (ie contains more than one page of text) it is advisable to provide a paper copy of the study to which students can refer as they complete the questions online or on-screen.

The following example, the 'Excellent Credit Card Company', was delivered to students in a Systems Modelling module at the University of Luton in 1999. The company description was presented to students in paper format, whilst the questions appeared on a series of screens (see Figures 4.12 to 4.15).

Excellent Credit Card Company

The Excellent Credit Card Company operates on the continent. It enables card holders to obtain petrol from pumps operating 24 hours per day by using the card in the same way we currently do in the UK for cash dispensing by swiping the card through a reader and entering a code. This records the card holder account number and any petrol obtained is charged to that account number by the pump computer. Charging is done overnight by modem to the online system at Excellent. At the end of transmission of charges, Excellent download any card numbers which have been reported as lost or stolen from a file of reported numbers. These will then no longer function at any pump which has been updated. So, at worst, one day elapses from notification before the card is cancelled.

When a customer first applies for a card by telephoning the enquiry line (in response to advertisements in the press), an application form is sent out. The application form requires the applicant to fill out personal details including bank name and address. On return of this form the bank is sent a request for credit rating together with a copy of the application form as authorisation. If a suitable reply is obtained, the form and credit rating is passed to the card unit.

The card unit allocates a unique PIN number from a file of available numbers and opens an account using a unique account number, again from a file of available numbers. The number is prefixed with the first letter of the client's surname. The customer's personal details and bank sort code account number are placed on the file. The account number is then passed to the card printing process.

The card printing process uses the information on the customer's account file to print a new card and the new PIN number on rice paper. The new card is mailed to the client and also under separate cover the PIN number. This arrives with strict instructions to memorise the number and eat the rice paper on which it is printed. To this end, the paper used has an attractive range of flavours.

The billing process for customers starts with the overnight transmission of charges from the pump computers. These transmissions are appended together as the night progresses to make a complete daily transaction file. At 6 a.m., when all transactions have ceased, each day's transactions are sorted into account number order and merged with the cumulative account transaction file which will be used to create the client statements for both garages and users.

Each day of the month, from the first day, one letter of the alphabet is taken in order and all clients with a surname starting with that letter have a statement prepared from the account transaction file. This is filed in client account number and date order and a copy sent to the client. The total and client account number is then forwarded to the direct debit unit for collection of moneys. Direct debit then use the customer account information to prepare direct debit transmissions to the client's bank. A copy of the transmission is maintained for seven years.

You may ignore the following:

1   How lost cards are reported and dealt with

2   How the garage information is created

3   How the garage is reimbursed

4   Archiving and file maintenance activities

You may assume the following:

1   That garages which participate are recorded on an account file with all relevant information having as key the garage account number. The mechanisms of this creation can be ignored.

2   The company maintains a file of details of all banks keyed by bank sort code.

3   The garage account and the client account files have on them their bank sort code account number.

4   Paper files include the customer application forms and the bank credit replies.

Figure 4.12 Case study

The module had successfully integrated CAA into its delivery and assessment methods. Students were familiar with the question types involved through a mixture of formative tests and self-assessment 'tasters' that were available throughout the term.

After completing a small number of MCQs on systems basics, students were asked to apply their knowledge to increasingly complex graphical material. They were also required to analyse the written materials prior to submitting a response.

Figures 4.13–4.15 show three of the computer-based questions that students were required to answer following their analysis of the 'Excellent Credit Card Company' case study. In Figure 4.13, the student has to select the appropriate term for each of the processes indicated on the diagram. (Each item P1–P5 contains a drop-down list of options – as shown with item P1 – from which the student selects the correct response.)

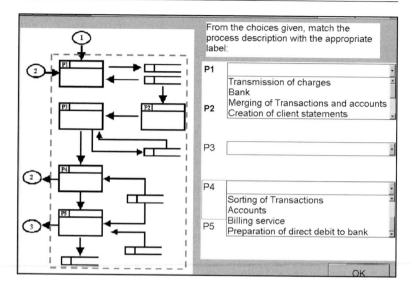

Figure 4.13 Process description question

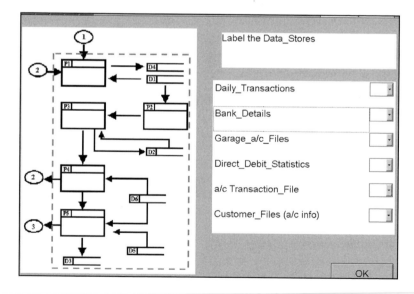

Figure 4.14 Data store question

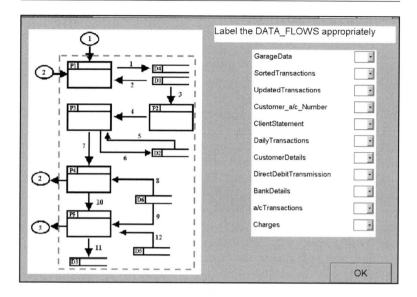

Figure 4.15 Data flows question

Note
Case study and the questions illustrated in Figures 4.13, 4.14 and 4.15 by Christine Steven.
Graphics and question construction by Ian Hesketh.

In Figure 4.14, the student must correctly identify each of the data stores indicated in the diagram (D1–D6). (As above, each part of the question contains a drop-down list with options D1–D6, from which the response is chosen.)

In Figure 4.15, the student must identify the data flows represented by the arrows labelled 1–12. Each part of the question now contains a drop-down list with options 1–12.

Beyond text

As multimedia (including graphics, animation, audio and video) has enhanced CAL, so it can improve CAA by increasing the range of possible question types, introducing interactivity and adding realism and authenticity to assessments. The inclusion of multimedia components can also promote student motivation, a particularly relevant feature when CAA is used for formative assessment. Multimedia applications are particularly well-suited to certain disciplines including language studies, music, media studies, and design, as well as many science-based subjects. Care must be taken, however, not to produce assessments that are overly or unnecessarily complicated.

Much has been written about the importance of realism and authenticity in higher education, and realistic assessment is as important as realistic teaching and learning (Dearing, 1997). Such assessments must be based upon students carrying out realistic tasks within a believable context. The creation of the context may range from the inclusion of embedded but discrete media items to the use of sophisticated simulators such as those used in the airline industry to test a pilot's ability to cope with emergencies (Whittington and Campbell, 1999).

The range of question types available in a typical CAA system has already been discussed. Many of the examples given are text-based but some allow for the incorporation of images and multimedia elements for illustrative purposes. For example, MCQs with an image included in the stem could require a student to identify an object or event. A typical instance from medicine is the University of Florida College of Medicine's Histology tutorial (http://www.medinfo.ufl.edu/year1/histo/accessed January 2003) which contains large numbers of microscope slides along with straightforward identification style questions.

Hotspot question types go a step further and ask the student to identify a particular region of an image. This leads to questions such as 'Identify the hypothalamus in this diagram of a human brain' or 'Where is this structure most likely to fail, given the load indicated by the arrows?' Such a style of question would also be appropriate for assessment in highly visual disciplines, such as art history.

Audio and video

Assessing a student's abilities with text is important, but in many disciplines it is desirable for graduates to be able to understand and synthesise information from a much wider range of sources (Bennett, 1998). The introduction of audio and video into assessment offers tutors a broader set of contexts in which to test students. In the arts, for example, an assessment of a student's appreciation of a play can include video of an actual performance. Similarly, historians are encouraged to study primary sources. In the twentieth century, these sources have included much more than text. A question about how the German perspective of blanket bombing differs from the British perspective could include some newspaper clippings, radio broadcasts and newsreel footage from the Second World War (adapted from Bennett, 1998).

Case studies can also be enhanced greatly with the use of multimedia.

In a study conducted at Strathclyde University, a set of social work case studies were introduced to students in a text-based format, and the students found the characters shallow and unbelievable. When digitised recordings of actors and actresses playing the various characters were added, the students' perception of the problems greatly improved, showing that through visual and aural impact, multimedia can enhance the process of understanding (Whittington and Campbell, 1999).

Care must always be taken to ensure that students with sensory impairments are not disadvantaged by the use of CAA. Adding multimedia to assessments can produce many advantages but can also raise unacceptable barriers. Subtitled videos and transcripts of audio clips should be included. Chapter 8 addresses further aspects of the use of multimedia in CAA.

Chapter 5

Feedback

In this chapter, we consider some issues surrounding the role of feedback in assessment and learning generally and ask what CAA can contribute to feedback processes. We then consider approaches to designing feedback for CAA and look at examples of different types of online feedback including predefined responses, model answers, online response to essays, and mixed-mode feedback.

Introduction: the politics of feedback

Feedback itself is a complex process and can mean many different things. Although it is generally thought of as 'good', Rowland (2000) and his co-researchers observe that feedback can be a means by which students develop their learning (or 'grow' in his biological metaphor) or it can be a means by which they are controlled. That is, it can help ensure that students' explorations always occur within specified parameters. Because feedback with CAA is often standardised and is usually automated, it is important to be alert to this second, potentially controlling, role of feedback.

In his discussion of the current poor state of summative assessment practices, Knight argues for the further development of formative assessment in curricula. He suggests that such assessment should 'engage students with feedback about their work in order to signal what else is valued in the curriculum, what might count as fair evidence of achievement in those terms and to indicate directions for further learning' (Knight, 2002b). His notion of formative feedback is that it would stimulate further discussions, and while such interactions might not be wholly conducted within CAA, it is possible that CAA could enable the first stage of such formative work.

What do we mean by feedback? Knight (2002a), citing Askew and Lodge (2000), identifies three categories of formative feedback:

1   Feedback 'as a gift from the teacher to students to help learning'.
2   Feedback which makes links between previous and current learning, 'integrating new knowledge and extending established schema'. Although more 'conversational' than the previous type, this category of feedback still sees the teacher in control and determining the agenda for the feedback.
3   Feedback as dialogue between teacher and student. Here a more equal relationship is obtained between teacher and learner.

Uses of CAA for feedback appear to fall into categories 2 and 3. With automated feedback, the lecturer determines the tone and content of feedback, thus setting the 'agenda'. However, as the example below from Laurillard *et al.* (2002) demonstrates, CAA can also facilitate feedback dialogues between learner and teacher and indeed learners and their peers.

Finally, current debates about the language and, indeed, politics of feedback are worth considering. Recent research in the area of academic writing suggests that students often do not understand the discourse of feedback (Lillis and Turner, 2001; Lillis, 2001; Higgins *et al.*, 2001) and in such cases, they learn very little from it. Although this research refers largely to essayistic literacy, it is nonetheless worth stressing that developing a shared understanding of the language of feedback is as significant as the medium by which it is delivered. This becomes particularly important when we consider more dialogic online feedback practices such as the use of email, computer-mediated communication (CMC) and electronic annotation.

What can CAA contribute to feedback practices?

One of the key purposes of formative assessment is to provide feedback to students to improve their learning. Ramsden (1992) argues that it is 'impossible' to overestimate the importance of timely feedback on students' progress, and he cites the use of computer-based assessment (CBA) as an 'excellent opportunity' to provide feedback swiftly. Indeed, two of the main strengths of CAA in feedback processes are the capacity (with automated exams) to respond quickly (feedback can be instantaneous) and the capacity to offer students unlimited attempts to practise and receive feedback.

Feedback in these instances may offer some or all of the following:

*   scores (of individual questions and entire assessment)
*   notification of the correctness of a response
*   written guidance, praise and study suggestions based on a student's response.

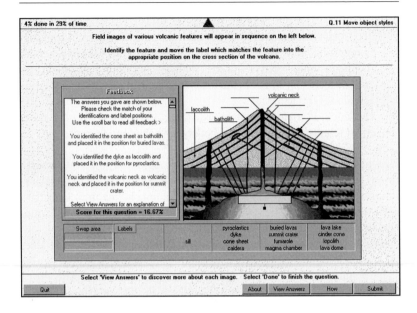

Figure 5.1 Immediate feedback from the TRIADS assessment system

Source: Question design and images by Dr Peter Regan and the Devil's Tower (volcanic pipe) in Yosemite by Dr Stan Salmon.

Additionally, CAA can mean that students can have access to feedback following summative examinations. As Race (1999) observes, traditionally, summative assessment tends to offer students only a minimal amount of feedback and this is a missed opportunity for learning. With CAA, following the logging of students' final responses, access can be given to the same test again with feedback options enabled. Thus, summative assessment can then become formative (Baggott and Rayne, 2001). Additionally, online environments allow for multimodal feedback: responses can combine text, image, sound, film etc. See, for example, Figures 5.1 and 5.2, from the TRIADS assessment system, which use photography and graphing techniques to provide feedback.

Furthermore, formative CAA can allow students to get things wrong and receive feedback in 'private'. It is often said of academic research that there is much to learn from projects that have gone awry, but that due to a culture of success in higher education, academics tend not to publish or speak about work which has 'failed'. Similarly, students potentially have much to learn from making mistakes (and receiving feedback) in assessment, and CAA, with its potential repeatability and anonymity, can enable

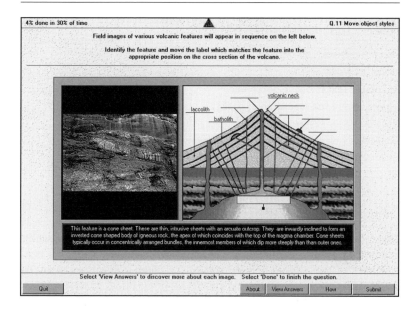

Figure 5.2 Feedback incorporating photographic images

Source: Question design and images by Dr Peter Regan and the Devil's Tower (volcanic pipe) in Yosemite by Dr Stan Salmon.

an environment in which such a 'rehearsal' is possible (Brown, 1999). Similarly, regular feedback can help build student confidence.

Finally, Knight (2002a), citing Palloff and Pratt (1999), argues that online learning enables more feedback from a greater number of sources – students, tutors etc. Technology 'enhances the feedback by capturing it for later consideration, whereas much face to face feedback is too fast to be captured or too complex to be properly appreciated …' See, for example, Baggott and Rayne (2001), which describes a molecular cell biology course in which formative and summative CAA is combined with peer-assessed, web-based posters and online conferencing. Feedback (both automated and discursive) is received from tutors and other students. In the latter instance, feedback is more or less synonymous with the dialogic interaction generated in computer-mediated communication. For Lea (2001), such interaction not only constitutes a form of peer feedback, but also functions as a component of assessment. Students are encouraged to incorporate the interaction with their peers generated in virtual learning environments within their own pieces of assessed writing. For a fuller consideration of the role of feedback and assessment in computer-mediated communication, see Chapter 8.

Table 5.1 Types of feedback in CAA

MCQ responses – automated two-stage feedback
Model answers
Annotated text in online documents
Expert system self-evaluation eg THESYS
Electronic peer review
Simulation – electronically generated response
Email or CMC responses

Designing feedback

There is a range of feedback types which can be either automatically generated or distributed and managed in CAA systems. Table 5.1 is a summary of these types and the rest of the chapter discusses many of these, while others are addressed elsewhere in the book.

Ultimately, CAA is simply a means by which feedback can be constructed and delivered to students. As with text-based or spoken feedback, it is *what* is said and *how* that is really important. The following section describes different uses of computers to provide feedback for students and offers suggestions and examples for designing computer-based responses.

Automated feedback – objective testing

Most CBA packages allow tutors to enter their own feedback, so that a message appears explaining to students why the response is right or wrong and perhaps directing them to relevant reading or course materials. Two-stage feedback is available in some software packages. In such models, specific information and suggestions for improvement are given based on the option that a student selected (Dalziel, 2001). Having read this feedback, the student then has the opportunity to choose further feedback on the topic. Additionally, some packages allow for the inclusion of hints to be made available during the test to help a student toward the correct answer. (Marks can be adjusted accordingly.) For example, the CUE assessment system (http://www.scrolla.ac.uk, accessed January 2003) allows questions to be divided into 'steps'. Students can choose to break the question down into several defined parts. Each question step provides some feedback and hints on answering. Students also have the opportunity to reveal answers as they progress.

The provision of feedback (particularly on incorrect responses) is especially useful when using CBA for formative and self-assessments. Feedback can take a variety of forms, ranging from a simple indication of correctness to suggestions about further study. The following are examples of different types of feedback:

- correctness of the response ('correct'/'incorrect')
- correct answer ('No, the correct answer is "compatibility"')
- why an answer is correct ('Yes, "dramatic monologue" is correct because it encompasses both voice and genre')
- directive feedback which tells the students where to find the correct answer ('See chapter 3 of *An Introduction to Economics*')
- non-directive feedback which prompts students with relevant hints ('Remember that "to be" is an irregular verb').

As mentioned above, the content of feedback should ideally be constructive and useful to the student in terms of future learning. Wholly negative feedback risks undermining student confidence and causing frustration with the CAA process (Bull and McKenna, unpublished research). Designers of feedback should also consider giving further information about correct responses.

Figures 5.3 and 5.4 show the alternatives for a particular question and the feedback, in this case a solution to the problem, that would appear (Wood and Burrow, 2002). Note that upon answering the question correctly, the student has the option of either selecting 'further study' or 'solution', or continuing with the assessment.

Model answers

Model answers offer another form of feedback for students and they can serve as a stimuli for comparison and reflection. In a text response, students can write their own answer and then click to reveal one or more 'model' responses. They can then discuss their own answer in relation to the example(s). In a study on the role of narrative in online learning resources, Laurillard *et al.* (2000) position this sort of feedback in the context of the conversational framework of learning (Laurillard, 1993), which sees learning as a series of dialogic interactions between student and teacher. In the particular experiment they describe, students working in small groups with an online learning resource were asked to generate a joint response using an online text editor. They then compared this with a 'model' answer and reflected on the differences between the two texts. Laurillard *et al.* argue that the answer served as a type of feedback in

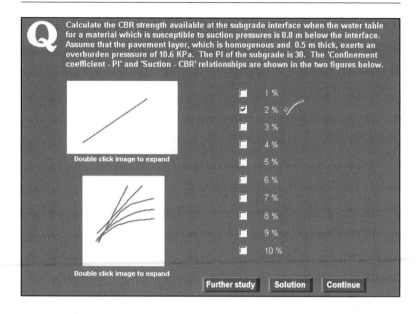

Calculate the CBR strength available at the subgrade interface when the water table for a material which is susceptible to suction pressures is 0.8 m below the interface. Assume that the pavement layer, which is homogenous and 0.5 m thick, exerts an overburden presssure of 10.6 KPa. The PI of the subgrade is 30. The 'Confinement coefficient - PI' and 'Suction - CBR' relationships are shown in the two figures below.

☐ 1 %
☑ 2 %
☐ 3 %
☐ 4 %
☐ 5 %
☐ 6 %
☐ 7 %
☐ 8 %
☐ 9 %
☐ 10 %

Double click image to expand

Double click image to expand

Further study   Solution   Continue

Figure 5.3 Example of a multiple-choice question used in Highway Drainage, from Wood and Burrows (2002)

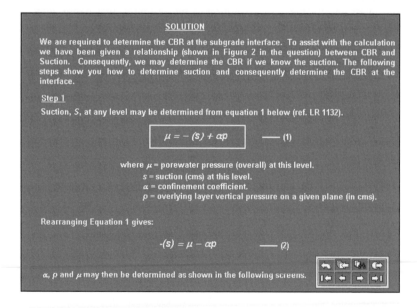

SOLUTION

We are required to determine the CBR at the subgrade interface. To assist with the calculation we have been given a relationship (shown in Figure 2 in the question) between CBR and Suction. Consequently, we may determine the CBR if we know the suction. The following steps show you how to determine suction and consequently determine the CBR at the interface.

Step 1

Suction, S, at any level may be determined from equation 1 below (ref. LR 1132).

$$\mu = - (S) + \alpha p \qquad (1)$$

where μ = porewater pressure (overall) at this level.
S = suction (cms) at this level.
α = confinement coefficient.
p = overlying layer vertical pressure on a given plane (in cms).

Rearranging Equation 1 gives:

$$-(S) = \mu - \alpha p \qquad (2)$$

α, p and μ may then be determined as shown in the following screens.

Figure 5.4 Solution to multiple-choice question, from Wood and Burrows (2002)

itself and motivated self-reflection on both topic and students' own performance.

Obviously, one potential risk with the use of model answers is to 'standardise' responses and perhaps appear to be implicitly discouraging innovative or original approaches to a question or topic. However, the use of multiple illustrative answers might help limit this risk, as could instructions which explain that a model answer is not necessarily the only 'correct' response.

Annotated text

Feedback which is not automatically generated, but which still makes use of technology, includes systems which enable a mix of standardised and personal comments to be electronically constructed and distributed to large groups, and software which allows readers to respond to student writing by marking a digital document. An example of the former is the Electronic Feedback Version 8 system, which enables tutors to construct and send feedback reports to students (Denton, 2001). These reports contain:

- general comments, which are addressed to the entire cohort being assessed;
- standard comments, which are 'stand-alone statements' about specific elements of the work that are selected as necessary during the marking process (for example 'You have failed to include an appropriate best fit line on your graph' (Denton, 2001); and
- personal comments which are addressed to the individual student (see Table 5.2 for an example).

It is claimed that this approach to feedback enables markers to respond to large groups more quickly and in more depth and that, because all discourse is wordprocessed, the feedback is more readable than hand-written comments.

Related feedback approaches to text-based assessment include the electronic annotation of written work, so that something approximating conventional marking practice takes place entirely online. One such technique would be to use a word processor's 'track changes' facility to provide online feedback or to use the 'comment' feature to create either text annotations or record audio messages; another would be to use an electronic stylus and tablet to 'write' on the student text. Stephens, Sargent and Brew (2001), in a survey of available software for non-automated assessment of written work, propose a model for an ideal

Table 5.2 Example feedback sheet produced in Normal Mode

FEEDBACK SHEET Created at 13.23pm on 18/03/01 Book 1

PACCH1004 Determination of a rate constant for the reaction of I^- and $S_2O_8{}^{2-}$ (aq)

Assessed by Phil Denton

STUDENT: Name

MARK: 24%

COMMENT:

The group generally completed this work to my satisfaction. That said, some of you made some elementary mistakes in your mole calculations.

Catherine, the quality of this work was very much below your usual standard. E-mail me if you need further assistance.

I have annotated your work with numbers and each number represents a particular comment. The numbers on your work have the following meanings:

3	Your axis is not numbered correctly. Always select chart type XY SCATTER when using MS Excel. (80%)
12	Lab reports should have the following sub-headings and should be presented in the following order; introduction, method, results, conclusion. (100%)
25	Your graph should display the individual data points in addition to a best fit line. The data points should NOT be joined together by a 'dot to dot' type line. (40%)
21	When comparing your results with value(s) from the literature, you should state the author, title, year, and publisher of any data sources you refer to. In this experiment $k_2 = 1.0 \times 10^{-2}$ mol^{-1} dm^3 s^{-1} (J. Chem. Ed. 1997, page 972). (40%)
4	Incorrect units/units not stated clearly. In this experiment, t in s, V in ml, k_1 in s^{-1}, k_2 in mol^{-1} dm^3 s^{-1} in ($V_{inf} - V$) is unitless. Correct units should be stated in all column headings and on graph axes. (60%)

Electronic Feedback 8. Licensed to Phil Denton until 30/06/02
Source: Denton, P. (2001) 'Generating and e-mailing feedback to students using MS Office', in Danson M. (ed.) Proceedings of the 5th International Computer-assisted Assessment Conference, 2–3 July 2001, Loughborough: Loughborough University. pp. 157–174 (accessed January 2003).

Note
The numbers in brackets after each comment shows you the percentage of students who required that comment..

'Integrated Marking Tool' which will combine nearly all of the above features such that markers could draw on an editable bank of feedback comments built up over time, provide personal responses to students, annotate electronic texts using symbols and handwritten suggestions, identify assessment categories, calculate marks and check for plagiarism. A feedback report would be transmitted online to students.

Mixed-mode feedback

Computers can also be used in conjunction with face-to-face teaching as a means of stimulating discussion and providing feedback to teachers and students. For example, the use of group support systems such as Teamworker have become increasingly popular as methods of group assessment. With such systems, students operate handsets (in much the same way as voting television studio audiences) to answer questions (usually of the multiple-choice variety). The breakdown of responses is then projected onto the screen in the form of a pie or bar chart (Irving *et al.*, 2000; Stuart, 2002). The nature and range of responses then form the basis of the participants' further discussion in the class. Additionally, as Stuart (2002) suggests, the lecturer is potentially better aware of the progress of large groups through the use of such systems.

Another example of mixed-mode feedback comes from the use of the Anaesthesia Simulator, which replicates conditions of an operating room and involves a computer-controlled mannequin which measures and records the students' capacity to administer anaesthesia and respond to different medical scenarios (Cleave-Hogg *et al.*, 2000) (see Chapter 8 for a full account of this simulation). Following the simulation, the student is rated by observing assessors and then meets with a supervisor for face-to-face feedback about the exercise.

In both of these examples, the use of CAA acts as a stimulus for other types of feedback and discussion with peers and teachers. Such a mixed-mode approach could also be taken using more basic forms of CAA. The automated assessment and feedback process could be used as a prelude to further interaction with tutors, essays, lab work, reflective writing, fieldwork etc.

Feedback in the curriculum

Feedback can take many guises and emanate from a number of sources – peers, self, teachers, examiners. It can be used for diagnostic reasons, to build confidence, to encourage wider reading and thinking on a subject and to give a particular steer to learning. While there are some limitations to using computers to generate and transmit feedback, it is the case that CAA systems enable quick feedback, even to large groups, and they have the capacity to provide feedback repeatedly and consistently.

Finally, it is worth reiterating Knight and Trowler's (2001) suggestion that feedback (particularly for formative assessment) should be explained to students at a programme level in order to foster an atmosphere in which it is understood and valued (cited in Knight, 2002a). Our own research bears out this need for a shared understanding about feedback between lecturers and students. We know of at least one instance in which, when faced with CAA self-assessments, students adopted what their tutors called a 'smash and grab' technique, 'punching any key' to 'strip off' the feedback and correct answers. When the lecturers realised that the students were using the CAA in a manner different to the reflective approach they had envisaged, the system was abandoned in favour of another CAA system which required students to work through complex pathways to solve problems (McKenna et al., in press). Lastly, it is worth remembering that CAA, even when operated anonymously by the student, provides lecturers with potentially rich feedback about their students' learning.

Chapter 6

Scoring and analysing objective tests

This chapter discusses the scoring of objective tests and ways of using statistical reports to analyse and improve questions and tests. Issues addressed include the use of question banks, adaptive testing, item analysis and statistics.

Introduction

All assessments should seek to be both valid and reliable, and there are many issues associated with test design and scoring which potentially influence reliability and validity. Validity ensures that a test measures what it intends to measure, and different forms of validity can be gauged using statistical techniques (Cronbach, 1949). Reliability ensures that this measurement is consistent; that is, you could repeat the assessment and achieve the same results. The two main measures of reliability are those of agreement between and within assessors, with the main threat to reliability being the lack of consistency of an individual marker (Brown *et al.*, 1997). CAA offers a particular advantage over paper-based assessments in that the computer is consistent in the marking of each assessment. This chapter does not provide a discussion of the conceptual issues of reliability and validity or a detailed description of the statistical techniques used to calculate them, although some of the statistics discussed in relation to item analysis below are relevant. Brown *et al.* (1997) discusses the concepts of validity and reliability in assessment in some depth, while Messick (1980), Moss (1994, 1995) and Gronlund (1988) provide an overview of the statistical techniques and issues surrounding the measurement of validity and reliability.

The format of an assessment will clearly have an impact upon validity, reliability and student performance. Various studies have attempted to ascertain the effects of variables such as question type and delivery mechanism (paper, machine-readable or computer-based). Outtz (1998) argues that the type of question(s), the mode in which the test is presented, type of response required and method of scoring all influence performance. Ward *et al.* (1980) analysed tests in two formats – multiple-response questions (optically scanned) and free response short answers – designed to assess undergraduate psychology students' problem-solving abilities. They concluded that the two versions of the test could not be considered equivalent. A similar study by Thissen *et al.*, (1994) of free response and multiple-choice questions for computer science and chemistry students revealed the different question types were testing different elements of students' performance. Finally, a study of the General Aptitude Test Battery, a US Employment Services Test, found that the examination method, which required candidates to make different types of mark for their answers on an optically scanned sheet, affected test outcomes. The requirement to indicate answers by filling in a circle below the options, rather than identifying correct answers by drawing a line within brackets, resulted in a slower test-taking speed and thus influenced their performance (Boyle, 1984). Fiddes *et al.* (2002) report no significant differences between students taking test on screen and on paper, but found that tests designed for screen delivery and printed out had a negative effect on student performance. Research has also investigated the validity of CAA in different disciplines. McGuire *et al.* (2002) found no difference between performance in a variety of mathematics tests on computer and paper, whereas Proctor and Donoghue (1994) found parity between objective tests and written examination performance in geography students.

It is not surprising that findings indicate that different question types test different skills (and abilities), as do different types of assessment in general. It is also important to recognise that much of the US research reported is based largely upon multiple-choice question-only tests, and many of the concerns are raised in relation to these being the main or sole determinants for university admission or employment selection.

Computer familiarity and anxiety are also considerations in relation to CAA test performance. A study of 1100 candidates in a computer-based test for teachers of English as a foreign language found no significant correlation between computer familiarity and test performance (Taylor *et al.*, 1998). Brosnan (1999), however, identifies that computer anxiety is an issue, though much of the research comparing computer-based and paper-based tests for anxiety effects is based in psychological testing situations rather than educational settings. The increasing use of computers in all sectors of education and society would suggest that computer anxiety and familiarity are diminishing factors. Indeed, some evidence suggests that teachers and academic staff may soon be overtaken in computing skills by their students. A survey of 6213 students from 399 Australian schools found that over half of them had 'a sound range of advanced information technology skills' (Meredyth *et al.*, 1999).

The remainder of this chapter explores issues surrounding the scoring of objective test questions, including guessing and negative marking, the role of item statistics, question banks, adaptive testing and associated statistical measures.

Scoring objective test questions

A standard and simple method of scoring responses is to allocate one or more marks for a correct response and no points for an incorrect one. Similarly, no marks would be awarded for an unanswered question. This works well with standard multiple-choice question types and where all the questions are of similar difficulty levels. However, within a test there may be some questions which are deemed more complex than others and therefore differential scoring may be employed depending on the perceived difficulty of a question.

The difficulty of a question is often predicted by the author of the question based on their knowledge of the material and perceived student ability level. Item statistics (discussed below) can also be used to determine more precisely the difficulty of a question.

For more complex question types (such as multiple-response or assertion/ reason) for which there may exist a range of correct or partially correct responses, scores can be assigned for different outcomes (see Figure 6.1). The creation of more sophisticated question types allows much greater complexity in scoring than traditional multiple-choice questions. For example, Figure 6.1 shows three different scoring options for a relatively simple multiple-response question. More complex question types, such as a drag and drop question with 12 different labels which must be correctly placed on a diagram, might involve a different score for each label, depending on its importance in the question. In addition, there may be some labels which are irrelevant to the question and therefore attract no marks. If there are random elements within the question, the possible scoring combinations increase further. It is therefore often difficult to directly compare the output of such assessments to those of traditional assessments, such as essays, where a holistic and very often limited range of marks are given. Mackenzie and O'Hare (2002) have found that tutors unfamiliar with the use of objective items are likely to place insufficient emphasis on scoring strategies, and, as a result, they are developing a Marking Simulator in order to promote better question design and results interpretation.

The following question is a multiple-response item. There are three correct responses to the question.

Which of the following are Irish poets? (Choose up to three responses.)

a   W. B. Yeats*
b   Carol Ann Duffy
c   Eavan Boland*
d   Robert Frost
e   Tony Harrison
f   Seamus Heaney*

* denotes correct responses

Score option 1

Response a, c, and f = 4 marks (1 score for complete correct answer)
All other combinations = 0 marks

Score option 2

Response with all three correct answers a, c and f = 4 marks
Response which includes two correct answers = 2 marks
Response which includes any one correct response = 1 mark
All others = 0 marks

Score option 3

A = +1
B = −1
C = +1
D = −1
E = −1
F = +1

This option corrects for guessing. Students should be advised that they will be penalised for choosing incorrect answers.

Figure 6.1 Examples of scoring a multiple-response item

Guessing and negative marking

A common anxiety about objective tests is that students will gain an inflated score simply through guessing. For example, with standard four-option multiple-choice questions students could, in theory, guess the correct answer to 25 per cent of the questions. In order to counteract this effect, negative marking is sometimes used. Negative marking is generally disliked by students and strongly debated by practitioners. Proponents of negative marking justify its use through the probability of students randomly gaining correct answers, and they argue that the benefit of negative marking is to make the test fairer for students who do not guess answers.

Negative marking can be applied in a variety of ways, including the following:

- cumulatively, where each negative mark contributes to the overall test score;
- within an individual question only (this is appropriate for more complex question types); and
- through corrective measures, such as guess correction applied post test.

Cumulative negative marking must be applied with care to ensure that students do not receive an overall negative score. For example, score option 3 in Figure 6.1 could result in a student receiving minus 3, which if repeated for other questions similarly scored could result in a very low examination mark. One possible solution would be to convert all negative question scores to zero. Another would be to use fractional scoring. For example, for a four-option multiple-choice question an incorrect response could be awarded minus 0.25, while the correct response would receive 1. Alternatively, the correct response could receive 3 marks and the incorrect responses minus 1.

Other more complex question types will require careful examination prior to instigating negative scoring to ensure that the overall effect does not penalise students. For complex question types, negative scoring for individual questions may be appropriate if, for example, the question is structured into several distinct sections requiring a number of responses. For further discussion of the issues of guessing and negative marking see Mackenzie and O'Hare (2002) and Burton (2001).

Guess correction

Alternatively, questions could be scored as normal, and a formula for guess correction could be applied at the end. A standard formula is

$$\text{SCORE} = R - \frac{W}{N-1}$$

R = the number of correct answers
W = the number of incorrect answers
N = total number of options per item (including the correct answer)

(Brown *et al.*, 1997)

So, if a student answered 35 questions correctly on a 50-question test in which each item had four options, the raw score after corrections would be calculated as follows:

$$\text{SCORE} = 35 - \frac{15}{4-1}$$

Score = 30

However, as suggested above, negative marking is a contentious issue, and some experts feel that corrective scoring is unnecessary if the assessment has been well-constructed with good coverage of course content and a sufficient number of questions of varying difficulty. It is worth remembering that the relevance of guessing decreases as the number of test items increases. If you have a true/false test containing *one* question, a student has a 50 per cent chance of getting it right and scoring full marks. The chances of scoring 100 per cent on a 45-question true/false test through random guessing are less than one in a trillion (10^{12}) and the chances of earning at least 70 per cent in a 45-question test are less than one in 300. Therefore the number of items in the test is important in the calculation of the impact of guessing (adapted from Heard *et al.*, 1997b).

Alternatively, as Brown *et al.* (1997) point out, intelligent guessing can be viewed as a useful skill that lecturers may wish to encourage. It should be recognised that there is a difference between blind guessing and informed guessing based on partial information, and while negative marking penalises students who are genuinely making random guesses, it is also penalising students who are making partially informed guesses.

Furthermore, evidence suggests that negative marking does not necessarily discourage students from guessing. Studies on negative marking from the 1940s (Cronbach, 1949) found that there was a tendency for students to select 'true' as a response to true/false questions rather than false. In addition, personality traits (risk-taking, submissiveness) were found to be important when employing penalties for guessing. A large-scale, blind comparative study undertaken by the Educational Testing Service (Angoff and Schrader, 1981) of 8500 students found slightly higher scores for competency tests where no negative marking was employed; however, only one of eight sub-tests was statistically significant, and no difference was found for subject matter tests. Timed tests magnified the scoring differences because negative marking schemes encouraged students to work more slowly. Higher ability students guessed more than lower ability students in tests without negative marking, and lower ability students omitted fewer items than higher ability students in negative-scored tests. This may indicate that confidence and an ability to follow instructions also have a bearing on the extent to which negative scoring has an impact upon test performance.

Traditionally, medical and veterinary examinations have employed negative marking for many of their examinations that are based on multiple-choice and true/false questions. However, the Royal College of Physicians has recently abolished negative marking on their Part One MRCP examinations (Royal College of Physicians, 2002) and the Royal Veterinary College has introduced a policy on objective testing advising against negative marking (Jacobs, 2002).

Confidence rating

An alternative approach, which is potentially powerful but little-used, is the adoption of confidence rating, which involves students identifying how confident they are that the answer they are selecting is the correct response. Gardner-Medwin, who developed the London Agreed Protocol for Teaching CAA system which incorporates confidence assessment, argues that with this approach students cannot do well by guessing, because they must either state 'low confidence' if they are guessing or else be heavily penalised each time they make an error. More positively, Gardner-Medwin suggests that confidence assessment both requires students to reflect on their reasoning for selecting answers and helps them develop judgement-making abilities (Gardner-Medwin, 1995). Davies (2002) identifies seven categories of student confidence, including those who know the answer definitely, those who may be unsure but can identify it from the options presented, those who guess and those who think they know the answer but are completely incorrect. Within a confidence-rated system, students can be asked to decide their level of confidence either prior to viewing the various answer options or after seeing the possible responses.

Scores are awarded according to the level of confidence expressed combined with the correctness of the response. Therefore, students who are very confident *and* select the correct response receive the highest score, while those who are very confident but incorrect receive the lowest score. Two examples of scoring strategies in use are shown in Table 6.1.

Davies' (2002) marking scheme was adapted from Gardner-Medwin (1995) following discussion with students who preferred a higher mark

Table 6.1 Scoring strategies for confidence rating

	Davies (2002)		Gardner-Medwin (1995)	
	Correct	Incorrect	Correct	Incorrect
Very confident	+4	−2	+3	−2
Fairly confident	+2	−1	+2	−2
Not confident	+1	0	+1	−1

for knowing the correct answer prior to display of the options, and no marks, rather than negative marks, for not being sure of the answer and ultimately answering incorrectly. For each of the score options in Table 6.1 there are associated negative scores, allowing reward for the selection of the correct response while differentiating between students with varying levels of confidence. Each response is awarded 4 marks, regardless of whether it is correct or incorrect.

For example: correct responses:

• 4 marks for a response, with 0 deducted because the student is correct and very confident.
• 4 marks for a response, with 2 deducted because the student is correct but only fairly confident.
• 4 marks for a response, with 3 deducted because the student is correct but not confident.

Incorrect responses:

• 4 marks for a response with 4 deducted because the student is incorrect and not confident.
• 4 marks for a response with 5 deducted because the student is incorrect and fairly confident.
• 4 marks for a response with 6 deducted because the student is incorrect and very confident.

Both Gardner-Medwin (1995) and Davies (2002) found that, statistically, confidence rating provided a more discriminating test of student ability when compared with tests where no confidence rating was applied. Student feedback also revealed that confidence rating had discouraged students from guessing and students felt they 'really had to think' when performing the confidence test (Davies, 2002).

If you do decide to use corrective scoring, it is important to alert students to this, so that they can alter their test-taking strategies accordingly.

Analysing assessments

One of the advantages of using CAA is that a variety of analyses can be automatically run to determine how well individual questions (and parts of questions) perform. This process is sometimes termed item analysis and generates item statistics. This information enables the lecturer to improve or eliminate weak questions (such as those that are too easy or difficult). Additionally, the performance of the test-takers (as a cohort and as individuals) can be analysed and this information can help the lecturer identify:

- general problem areas within the course or module
- students who are struggling
- students who perhaps are not being sufficiently challenged.

Table 6.2 shows how the results of frequent objective testing can be used to identify possible problems with student performance. An extract from a spreadsheet recording the results of a group of sociology students in a weekly multiple-choice test designed to reinforce lecture material is shown, with an explanation of the inferences which can be drawn from this data.

While analysis can be done by hand, the time required to analyse marks and overall grades can be a deterrent. Generally, CAA software packages designed for summative assessment automate this process and include a reporting facility which generates a range of statistical analyses on the performance of both the test-takers and the questions. It is often possible to produce reports that compare individual and group performance as well as question statistics which indicate the quality of the questions. Question (or item) statistics are useful for many pedagogical purposes, which are explored in further detail in the section on item analysis below, and they can help classify questions for use in question banks and adaptive testing. Figure 6.2 provides an example of the type of statistics which can be generated from CAA software.

Although testing organisations, such as examination boards and psychometricans, routinely use sophisticated item statistics to construct and validate banks of tests, their use in higher education assessment is not yet common. The remainder of this chapter discusses item statistics in

Table 6.2 Sample analysis of student performance based on regular MCQ tests

Students	Week number and assessment scores (percentage)						
	1	*2*	*3*	*4*	*5*	*6*	*7*
A	57	63	21	35	40	27	20
B	68	71	45	79	83	80	77
C	23	21	11	0	0	0	0
D	45	51	45	79	83	80	77
E	0	0	0	0	0	0	0
F	63	0	51	0	47	0	35
G	54	58	35	50	58	60	62

The pass mark is 40 per cent.

Sample analysis of the results
The table provides a great deal of additional information about students A–G over the seven-week period. Student A's performance has diminished steadily over the seven-week period and is a cause for concern. Most people would share the view that Student B is one we have little to worry about. Student C, however, has failed the first three tests and after Week 4 has failed to undertake any assignments at all. This is a student we would need to look for and investigate. Student D was not doing well to start with but after Week 4 is achieving results identical to those of Student B. This is indeed a cause for concern and suggests either a case of advanced telepathy or cheating! Most tutors would recognise Student E as one who causes a great deal of work. Is this student on the course or did he or she drop out at an early stage? Student F obviously has a problem. It seems likely that this student is either doing a part-time job on alternate weeks or is suffering from the 'cheap British Rail fares on Thursdays' syndrome and is therefore missing Friday afternoon classes. At the same time this student's test scores are diminishing rapidly so she or he needs a great deal of attention. After a glitch in Week three, student G is making steady progress.

Example from 'Strategies for Diversifying Assessment in Higher Education', Oxford Centre for Staff and Learning Development, Oxford Brookes University, 1994.

general and the applications of question banks and adaptive testing, before providing a brief overview of the methods and issues associated with item statistics.

Item statistics

Item (or question) statistics measure the characteristics of each question, indicating its worth for inclusion in a test or bank of questions. There are two key methods of obtaining item statistics – classical test construction and latent trait analysis. Classical test construction provides a simple, although limited, method of evaluating a test. Latent trait analysis (both

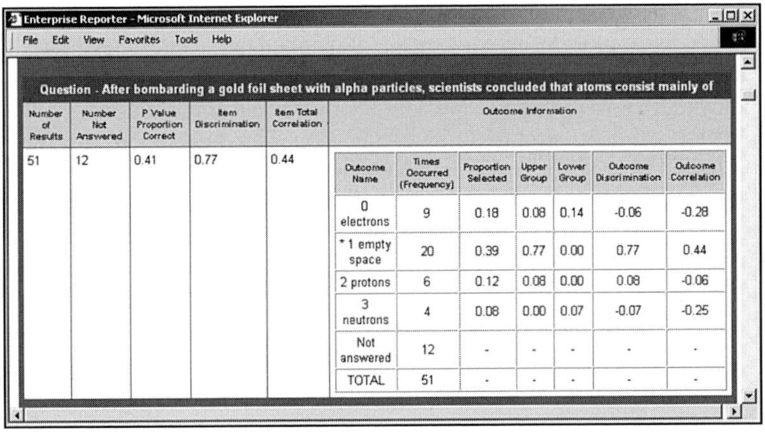

Number of Results	Number Not Answered	P Value Proportion Correct	Item Discrimination	Item Total Correlation
51	12	0.41	0.77	0.44

Outcome Information

Outcome Name	Times Occurred (Frequency)	Proportion Selected	Upper Group	Lower Group	Outcome Discrimination	Outcome Correlation
0 electrons	9	0.18	0.08	0.14	-0.06	-0.28
* 1 empty space	20	0.39	0.77	0.00	0.77	0.44
2 protons	6	0.12	0.08	0.00	0.08	-0.06
3 neutrons	4	0.08	0.00	0.07	-0.07	-0.25
Not answered	12	-	-	-	-	-
TOTAL	51	-	-	-	-	-

Figure 6.2 Example of Item Analysis Report from Question Mark Perception, Enterprise Manager

Source: Questionmark, http://www.questionmark.com

Rasch analysis and item response theory) takes the unit of analysis as the individual question and involves a more complex estimation of up to three parameters. Although it can seem time-consuming, item analysis provides a rich source of information about assessments.

The statistics generated by both these methods can be used to gather detailed information about the questions themselves and can potentially provide feedback to both student and teachers and aid curriculum design. The statistical data generated allows an evaluation of the quality of the questions, and may point to potential improvements. For example, a question which is answered correctly by 90 per cent of a student group would probably be felt to be too easy, because it does little to differentiate between the able and less able students. Furthermore, if none of the students in a group choose two of the five options for a question, it is likely that these options are implausible and are weakening the question. Additionally, statistical measures may alert test designers to questions that may result in differential performance of a sub-group of students. For example, females may outperform males of similar ability in performing a specific skill. Question statistics can be used to record the performance of a sub-group and inform quality control: if an item is found to be discriminating on an invalid basis it should be withdrawn or modified prior to inclusion in a test (McAlpine, 2002a). Furthermore, statistical data generated can offer both students and lecturers a detailed picture of the performance of an individual student. This type of feedback can be very positive in terms of motivating and enhancing student learning. It can inform students of specific strengths and weaknesses and evaluate their progress in relation to the course objectives and their peers. At the level of a course or programme, question statistics can be usefully employed to help determine future curriculum design and development. They may also help to identify where further resources are needed, for example, to address an area of common student weakness. Lastly, it should be noted that formative and summative tests may produce different question statistic profiles. For example, a formative test which allows multiple attempts (prior to recording of the percentage of correct responses) is likely to show a higher correct response rate than the same item used in a summative test which allows only a single attempt.

The following sections consider question banking, adaptive testing and provide a basic overview of some of the statistics which may be used in classical test construction and latent trait analysis. As mentioned at the outset of the chapter, a detailed and comprehensive analysis of statistical techniques associated with question banking and adaptive testing is beyond the scope of this book; however, several texts are recommended for further detail, including Wright and Bell (1984), McAlpine (2002a), Wainer (2000), Choppin (1979) and Hambleton *et al.* (1991).

Question banks

Question (or item) banks are collections of questions which allow the rapid and reliable creation of customised tests for precise and multiple aims.

Question banks are usually developed according to a definable subject area. Within the framework of a bank, questions can be grouped according to difficulty, the type of skill being tested (such as recall, comprehension, analysis or application) and the specific topic addressed. Assessments can then be designed which draw a certain number of questions from the bank, thereby ensuring that specific skills and levels of competence will be examined. For example, a lecturer might wish to construct an assessment of a certain level of difficulty which tested students' capacity to identify and analyse cell structures in human biology. Questions which qualified according to difficulty and topic could then be automatically selected. In order to contribute to a variety of tests, questions within a bank must be uniquely identifiable and described as fully as possible. Each question is independent of the others and able to be withdrawn according to different test requirements, while additional questions can be added. Figure 6.3 provides an example of how a question bank might be represented graphically. Reviewing the designation of items as easy or difficult can

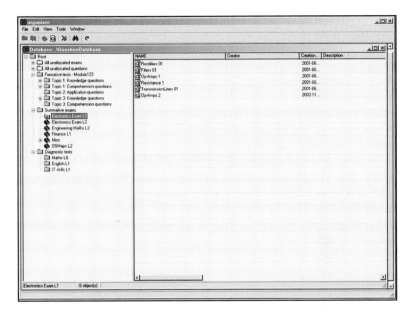

Figure 6.3 Example of a question bank structure, from I-assess software

Source: EQL International, http://www.i-assess.co.uk

help to inform both teaching and assessment activities, in particular to provide targeted formative feedback and learning support (Maughan *et al.*, 2001).

Item banking is most commonly associated with latent trait analysis (see below), as it is desirable to measure each question individually (rather than as part of a test, which is the approach adopted for classical test construction). However, classical statistics can still be useful in the construction of item banks.

Gaining a measure of the quality of a question through the generation of item statistics prior to inclusion in a bank ensures valid and reliable tests are constructed. By adopting common approaches to defining the features of a question (both statistical and pedagogical), a bank becomes a re-useable, shareable resource which, if created using latent trait analysis, can also be used for adaptive testing. Latent trait analysis is used to provide a model for what should happen when a student attempts an item (Rasch, 1980). However, the models allow for variation between what is expected and what is achieved, as some students do not learn in the way which we might expect them to.

In most banks, items are calibrated once, often by pre-testing with a sample group. CAA systems can allow the dynamic calibration of items, which means that each time a question is attempted within a bank, data is gathered and added incrementally, building a fuller and more accurate analysis of the item (McAlpine, 2002b). This may result in a new difficulty level being assigned to the question and may help to inform discussion about standards as well as content and pedagogy. An advantage of dynamic calibration is that incremental adjustments to an item bank are made in line with any adjustments in the curriculum. Care needs to be taken over the recalibration of new items as this will have a disproportionate effect on their value and, consequently, their assigned difficulty level.

As suggested in the previous section, caution also needs to be taken with item banks that contain both formative and summative questions, as student approaches to formative and summative assessment vary. It is likely that formative assessment, particularly self-assessment, is taken less seriously and influences the way in which questions are answered and their resulting item statistics.

Adaptive tests

Computer adaptive testing (CAT) is a sophisticated method of CAA in which the computer determines the range of questions asked according to the test-taker's ability. The principle behind CAT is that an efficient measurement of a student's ability can be gained by customising the assessment according to the student's performance. Successive questions are chosen from a large bank categorised according to content and difficulty. Questions are selected according to the candidate's responses to previous questions; therefore, the student receives fewer questions that are either too hard or too easy and this speeds up the testing process. The test ends when the student's ability has been evaluated to a required level of accuracy.

A number of advantages and disadvantages for CAT are reported in the literature (Rudner, 1998; Green, 1983; Wainer, 2000). Many of these – such as faster reporting and administration, the need for computer resources and student familiarity with computers and software – are generic to CAA. Where CAT does offer benefits is in presenting each student with an individual test. This deters cheating in large-scale formal testing and offers flexible, secure testing on demand. In addition, testing times are reduced, as students are not presented with inappropriate questions and the test is ended once their ability level has been determined. It would appear that the greatest disadvantage is the resources required to create and maintain a calibrated item bank. However, as McAlpine (2002b) asserts, CAT offers the opportunity to make assessment maximally efficient and appropriate to the student. In addition, she argues that CAT can contribute to learning more widely by automatically generating learning resources relevant to students' needs and facilitating student-led curricula (McAlpine, 2001).

Computer adaptive testing is increasingly used in the US. Drasgow and Olson-Buchanan (1999) report some interesting applications across educational and training sectors, demonstrating the cost and time savings as well as raising implementation and pedagogical issues, such as the use of item response theory, pedagogical design of question banks in different topics, delivery and incorporation of multimedia. The Educational Testing Service (ETS) has used CAT for the Graduate Record Exam (taken by all candidates for postgraduate study in American universities) since 1994 and has delivered over 1 million CATs since then.

The following sections provide a basic overview of some of the statistics which may be used in classical test construction and latent trait analysis.

Classical test construction

Classical test construction (or classical test theory) is widely used in the UK and is based on psychological assumptions about candidate ability which have been refined over time to accommodate aspects of educational testing. Ability in terms of classical test construction is defined as 'the expected value of observed performance on the test of interest' (Hambleton *et al.*, 1991). There are two main item statistics undertaken in classical test construction – discrimination and facility. There is also a range of other indicators of question (item) performance which can be taken into consideration.

As with many statistical measures, there are both positive and negative aspects to their use. A number of issues have been raised regarding the use of classical test construction, many of which led to the development of more sophisticated educational measurement tools, such as latent trait analysis. In particular, classical test construction results in:

- the ability of the candidate being determined by the difficulty of test. Therefore, if a test is difficult, students appear to have a lower ability than when a test is easy;
- the features of particular questions being determined by the group of students taking the test. This makes it problematic to construct tests for a wide group of mixed ability students.

However, classical test construction has much to offer in informing lecturers about the quality of their question, tests and students, both individually and as a group. It is worth remembering that, although possible, it is rare that such analysis of the quality of assessment is conducted for paper-based assessments. The following sections provide a basic overview of some of the statistics which may be used in classical test construction and latent trait analysis.

Discrimination

Discrimination helps to measure the power of an individual question to discriminate between the stronger and weaker students. It does so by looking at the correlation between the performance of a sub-group of students on a particular question and their overall scores on the assessment. There are a number of formulae for calculating discrimination; the most common is the Pearson product-moment correlation between the item and total test score. There are a number of forms for Pearson's product-moment correlation and the appropriate formula for educational measurement from McAlpine (2002) is given below:

$$rxy = \frac{\sum xy}{NsxSy}$$

where:

rxy = the correlation between the item (x) and the test total (y)
xy = the sum of the products of the deviations of the items and the totals
N = the number of observations
sx = the standard deviation of the item
Sy = the standard deviation of total marks

The application of the formula can depend upon the structure and purpose of the test. If all the questions in a test are seeking to measure one content area or specific skill, then the correlation between the item and the total test score minus that item would be appropriate. If the test is measuring several content areas, divided into sections within the test, then the correlation between an item and the other items in that section would be suitable. If a test is composed of questions each seeking to measure a different skill area or specific area of knowledge, it is likely that the correlation between an item and other external performance measures (for example, previous relevant coursework marks) would be most useful.

A simpler method (Brown et al., 1997) looks at the number of correct responses to an item by the top and bottom thirds of the test-takers (ranked according to their overall score on the assessment).

$$D = \frac{(H - L)}{N}$$

or

$$D = (H - L) \div N$$

D = discrimination
H = number of correct responses to question by the top third of test takers
L = number of correct responses to question by bottom third of test takers
N = number of students in the sub-group

If a test is taken by 90 students and 25 students in the top third answer the question correctly while only 10 students in the bottom third respond correctly, the discrimination of the question would be

$D = (25{-}10)/30$
$D = 15/30$
$D = 1/2$ or 0.5

Discrimination scores range from −1 to +1. Positive scores of +0.2 are generally accepted as the lowest boundary for good quality questions, with values above 0.4 indicating good discrimination (Massey, 1995). Negative scores indicate a question with a poor discrimination. Questions with a negative discrimination should be eliminated.

Facility

Facility measures the difficulty of a question and ranges from 0 to 1:0 being very difficult – with no one getting the answer correct – and 1 meaning that all test-takers responded correctly.

The following formula can be used to determine the facility of an item

$$Fac(X) = \frac{\overline{X}}{X \, \text{max}}$$

where:

$Fac(X)$ = the facility of question X
$\overline{X}$ = the mean mark obtained by all candidates attempting question X
$X \, \text{max}$ = the maximum mark available on the question.

The desired facility for a question depends to an extent on the value of marks attached to it within a test. If a question is worth a high proportion of the total marks of the test, it is desirable that the facility is close to 0.5; however, if a question is worth, for example, 2 marks out of a possible 100, it is acceptable for it to have a higher or lower facility value. If a test is composed of many questions, each with a low number of marks assigned to them, then a range of facility values would be acceptable. This would ensure that the abilities of strong and weak students are being tested. It is generally not desirable to have facility values above 0.85 or below 0.15 (McAlpine, 2002a). Overall, facility values on a test should balance out to an average facility of 0.5.

Additional indicators of item performance

Additional measures can be used to determine the performance of items within a test; these include standard deviation, reliability, standard error of measurement and frequency analysis. The standard deviation looks at the spread of the questions and a high standard deviation indicates that the test is spreading candidates out effectively, which may be desirable if item discrimination is good. Reliability considers the internal consistency of a test and can be measured in a variety of ways, with desirable levels depending on the type of assessment. Standard error of measurement is used in item response theory (IRT), while standard error of estimation is used in classical test theory. Both are calculated according to the number and quality of test items and the match between item difficulty and student ability. Frequency analysis measures the number of times a question (where appropriate) or alternative was selected. If students are allowed choice over the questions they answer, this can affect the way in which questions are marked. Although this is less relevant for CAA than examiner-marked tests, it may indicate that certain questions are attracting students of a specific ability range. Similarly, if certain distracters for objective tests are rarely chosen, they may be ineffective. Replacing them with more challenging alternatives may result in an improved facility or discrimination for the question. Examining the frequency of incorrect option choice can also help identify common misconceptions about a particular topic.

Latent trait analysis

Latent trait analysis (or theory) was developed to provide models that solve some of the problems identified with classical test construction and, in particular, it is designed to produce item characteristics that are independent of the group of students who took the tests. As latent trait analysis assumes that there is only one specific ability (or trait) being tested and that each item is independent of all the others in a test, items are considered apart from the test as a whole and of the candidates who take the test. Because the question difficulty is not determined by a group of students but by the item itself, it is comparable with other items which were not in the test but of the same difficulty. This means that a student's performance can be compared across tests with different questions because the item difficulty is determined independently of any particular test or cohort. This feature is called the *invariance* of item and ability parameters (McAlpine, 2002a). Invariance allows latent trait analysis to be used to support large-scale item banking, adaptive testing and analysis of item bias. There is debate, however, as to the extent to which questions can only be testing one ability and the extent to which they are treated independently by students (Lord, 1970).

IRT presents a series of models which are useful in the design and construction of tests. During the 1980s, IRT became an area of interest for professionals involved in test development and delivery using latent trait analysis. Three basic models have been developed using one, two and three parameters respectively. Each of the models allows variability of different factors:

- *one-parameter model*   variation in difficulty only
- *two-parameter model*   variation in difficulty and discrimination
- *three-parameter model*   variation in difficulty, discrimination and probability.

Rasch analysis is similar to IRT in that it provides a measurement of the ability of students in terms of the singular trait underlying the test. Rasch provides each item with a difficulty parameter and also gives a person parameter termed 'ability' – which is used in conjunction with the difficulty value to determine the likelihood of a student achieving the correct answer to a specific item. The model is based on the interaction of each person of a set ability, with each item of a specific difficulty.

For greater detail and fuller discussion of classical test construction and latent trait analysis, see texts by McAlpine (2002a), Hambleton, Swaminathan and Rodgers (1991) and Choppin (1979).

Pre-testing questions

It is advisable to pre-test questions before they are incorporated into examinations and/or question banks.

A pre-test of questions would normally be taken by students who are representative of those who will be taking the actual assessment. Students can be asked to record their start and finish times. (If using CBA, this can be done automatically.) Following the pre-test, the facility and discrimination of the individual items can be analysed, or, if appropriate, more sophisticated statistical analysis could be carried out. Lecturers might also wish to analyse the frequency with which distracters within items are chosen and replace those which are selected infrequently with more plausible options. Analysis of the pre-test may also provide useful feedback on the module or course itself, by highlighting areas of difficulty.

One strategy for pre-testing would be to use questions one year as part of a formative assessment, the score of which would not affect the student's module mark. After analysing and modifying the questions, they could be used the following year as part of a summative assessment.

If pre-testing is not possible, ensure questions are free of ambiguity and that the instructions (particularly for more advanced question types, such as assertion-reason) are clear. Pre- or 'beta'-testing of questions is a technique which can be used once you engage in a regular programme of objective testing. This involves including new questions in an assessment with known 'good' questions. After the students have taken the assessment, the facility and discrimination values of these questions are evaluated. If these indicators suggest that the questions are good, they can be included as part of the assessment. If not, the scores are omitted from the results.

Chapter 7

Constructing tests

This chapter offers suggestions on how to analyse the assessment methods in a module and how to examine the coverage, in terms of learning levels, in any single assessment. The authors would like to thank Jane Magill, University of Glasgow and Derek Stephens, Loughborough University, for their contributions to case study material.

Matching assessment methods to learning outcomes

Before writing objective test questions, it is useful to analyse the proposed subject area and assessment options for a course/module and determine *what* and *how* you wish to assess. When considering the introduction of objective testing, one possible approach would be to identify the learning outcomes of a module and determine which components, if any, can be assessed using this method. By integrating objective assessment with other methods, it is likely that a broader range of topics, abilities and levels of understanding will be assessed.

Prior to organising your assessment, briefly analyse your question material according to course content, difficulty, learning level, assessment type and question style (see Tables 7.1 and 7.2, for example). Such a breakdown of assessment components can help you identify potential areas of low coverage and unequal spread – either in terms of subject or question type.

Additionally, consider the student profile for the module:

- Will the students come from varying academic backgrounds (for example, from different fields of study into an interdisciplinary module or course)?
- Will some need more practice than others in certain areas?

Table 7.1   Assessment plan for An Introduction to Poetry (year 1)

Topics for assessment	Assessment methods (✓indicates the suitability of the method for each topic)			
	Objective testing	Critical comparison of two poems	Essay response	CAL manuscript study assignment
Knowledge of poetic terms associated with register, imagery, rhythm and form	✓✓✓ (Lecturer can ensure students answer questions on all terms)	✓✓	✓✓	✓
Application of poetic terms and concepts	✓✓✓ As above	✓✓	✓✓✓	✓
Understanding of historical development of genre	✓✓	✓	✓✓✓	✓
Ability to critically compare two poems	✓	✓✓✓	✓✓	NA
Understanding of poetic process from manuscript to publication	✓	NA	✓✓	✓✓✓

- Do you need to know what their knowledge base is before the module begins?
- Would it be useful to receive feedback as the term progresses on the extent to which students understand the material?

If the answer is yes to any of the above, then using objective tests for diagnostic and formative assessments might be useful.

Example assessment analysis – Understanding Poetry

Tables 7.1 and 7.2 show assessment breakdowns for 'An Introduction to Poetry', a 12-week, first year, undergraduate module. The lecturer wishes to assess the students in the following areas:

Table 7.2 Sample objective assessment on imagery – 35 questions

Topic	Bloom's Learning Levels – Number of questions					
	Knowledge	Comprehension	Application	Analysis	Synthesis	Evaluation
Metaphor	1	2	2	2		
Symbol	1	2	2			
Personifi-cation	1	1	2	2		
Synecdoche	1	1	1	1		
Defamiliar-isation	1	2	1	2		
Genre – haiku, imagist poem etc	1	2	2	2		

- knowledge and application of critical terms and theories across a number of topics;
- awareness of the process of development of a poem from manuscript form to publication;
- ability to write a critical comparison of two poems;
- general understanding of the historical development of poetry.

The lecturer has to plan the assessments with the following issues in mind:

- The cohort will be large (approximately 140 students).
- The previous experience of the students will be mixed; some may not have formally studied poetry before.
- For some, the module is an elective: they do not intend to take their study of literature further.
- For others, the module is a prerequisite for second and third year literature modules.

These characteristics (typical of level 1 modules in many disciplines) influence the assessment profile in several ways. The relatively large student numbers limit the number of free text assessments (such as essays or critiques) that can be reasonably marked. The mixed experience levels mean that the lecturer cannot assume previous knowledge of critical concepts in the subject and may wish to supply self-assessment and formative exercises to those who need extra help. Because the module is a prerequisite for higher level modules, it is desirable to determine, through assessment, that a core set of critical terms and concepts have been understood.

Table 7.1 shows how objective testing can be used as one of four assessment methods for this module, and identifies which methods are best suited to different topics.

The objective tests for the module may be formative, diagnostic and summative. A sample breakdown of an objective assessment is shown in Table 7.2.

The assessment on imagery shown in Table 7.2 could be taken by the students after a two-week session on the topic. By analysing the results of the test, the lecturer could determine whether students understand the relevant terms and concepts. Furthermore, such an assessment requires all students to answer questions on all topics. If objective testing were eliminated from the above assessment profile, it would be possible for students to avoid being assessed on entire sections of the module through tactical selection of essay questions.

Example assessment analysis – Business Planning and Marketing

Table 7.3 is an assessment analysis for 'Business Planning and Marketing', a 12-week, second year, undergraduate module. The lecturer wishes to assess the students in the following areas:

- knowledge and application of critical terms and concepts in business planning and marketing;
- ability to analyse business problems in for-profit and not-for-profit contexts;
- capacity to work with colleagues to research and present a successful marketing strategy;
- application of marketing principles to company case study.

As with the previous example, the cohort for this module is large and the students' experience of the topic varies widely. The lecturer wishes to use CAA both to deliver diagnostic testing at the start of the module, and as a programme of regular testing (which will contribute to the overall mark) throughout the module. Additionally, computer-mediated communication (CMC) will be used to supplement a group presentation in the assessment of students' capacity to work with colleagues in the planning and presentation of a successful marketing strategy.

As before, Table 7.3 shows how CAA can be used as one of five

Table 7.3 Assessment plan for Business Planning and Marketing

Topics for assessment	Assessment methods (✓ indicates the suitability of the method for each topic)				
	CAA objective test	Computer-mediated communication	Report	Essay response	Group presentation
Knowledge of relevant terms	✓✓✓	✓	✓✓	✓✓	✓✓
Application of critical concepts	✓✓✓	✓	✓✓	✓✓✓	✓✓
Ability to analyse business problems	✓	✓✓	✓✓✓	✓✓✓	✓✓
Application of marketing principles to case study	✓✓	NA	✓✓	✓✓✓	NA
Capacity to work with peers to plan and present successful marketing strategy	NA	✓✓✓	NA	NA	✓✓✓

assessment methods for this module, and it identifies which methods are best suited to different topics.

Example assessment analysis – Electronic Materials and Devices

This example describes the assessment for a level 3 course in 'Electronic Materials and Devices'. The course is a compulsory part of the four-year Bachelor of Technological Education degree at the University of Glasgow. Students of this degree programme take courses in a broad range of engineering subjects in addition to the Professional Studies courses that will qualify them to teach technology in schools. Students on this course come from a broad spectrum of educational backgrounds and many are mature students. Most of the students have not encountered material in this subject area although it builds on knowledge attained in other courses, such as a level 2 course in Materials. While the subject matter covered is not an essential component of the school curriculum, it is an important insight into state-of-the-art technology that is used by everyone. Past experience has shown that most students do use the knowledge gained in their future teaching careers. A few students have taken either permanent or vacation employment that uses the knowledge gained in this course. A wide range of assessment methods is used to best realise the potential of the varied student body, to encourage continuous participation in the course and encourage use of the knowledge beyond the university environment.

There are five components to the assessment:

1 *Computer-based tests* Two tests, each of 20 minutes duration, containing about 15 questions delivered and marked online. One test is carried out at the end of each part of the course.
2 *Traditional examination* A two-hour examination containing short compulsory questions and a choice of long questions.
3 *Tutorial questions* Four problem sets posed at regular intervals and handed in for marking. A tutorial follows each submission, with worked answers and explanations given. Students are encouraged to collaborate.
4 *Group study session* A group exercise to study in detail one area in current semiconductor technology. Results are presented as a group summary report of the topic.
5 *Laboratory exercise and report* Laboratory practical experience for each student to make and test a semiconductor device. Results are presented as a short evaluation and analytical report of their own device.

An assessment plan for the course is shown in Table 7.4. The computer-based tests are summative, and an example of the learning levels assessed for one example test is given in Table 7.5.

Timing

One of the potential strengths of objective tests is that they enable a relatively large number of questions to be asked in one assessment, thereby increasing the coverage of topics. However, when writing a test, the designer should be careful to allow enough time for the well-prepared student to complete the test, particularly if it includes complex questions which require a large amount of reading. One way of resolving this problem is to present a case study about which several questions are asked.

Table 7.4 Assessment plan for Electronic Materials and Devices (year 3)

Topics for assessment	Assessment methods (✓ indicates the suitability of the method for each topic)				
	CAA objective test	Traditional examination	Tutorial questions	Group study session	Laboratory exercise and report
Know the basic components and steps in fabrication of a device	✓✓✓	✓✓✓	✓✓	✓	✓
Apply simple device theory, predict device performance	✓✓✓	✓✓✓	✓✓✓	✓	✓✓✓
Make and test a simple device	NA	NA	NA	NA	✓✓✓
Understand and apply economics of manufacturing design	✓✓	✓✓	✓✓✓	✓✓✓	NA
Understand the variation and applicability of different device designs	✓	✓✓	✓✓	✓✓	✓
Use basic knowledge to design a device for a specific function	✓✓	✓✓	✓✓✓	✓	✓

Note
Table by Jane Magill, University of Glasgow.

As a general rule, the time allowed for an objective test should not exceed 90 minutes. Typically, 50–60 items are presented in an hour-long exam at undergraduate level 1. However, if you are examining higher levels of learning than recall, then plan for no more than 40 items per hour. Pre-testing the questions will help you gauge the time needed to complete them.

Table 7.5 Sample objective assessment on semiconductor fabrication
(15 questions)

Topic	Bloom's Learning Levels – Number of questions					
	Knowledge	Comprehension	Application	Analysis	Synthesis	Evaluation
Manufacturing process economics	1	2	1			
Chemistry of semi-conductors	1		1	1		
Properties of materials	1	1	1	1		
Process and device design	1	1	1		1	

Note
Table by Jane Magill, University of Glasgow.

Question order

Grouping like items

When assembling the test, you might wish to group similar items together.
Items can be grouped according to:

- question type (MCQ, T/F, text match etc)
- measurement of learning level (knowledge, comprehension, application, analysis etc)
- subject matter.

It is also advisable to arrange questions in order of increasing difficulty;
this sequencing gives students confidence at the early stages of the
section and prevents weaker students from spending too much time on
difficult items.

Test-item sequencing

There is conflicting evidence about the extent to which the sequencing of
questions relative to the order in which the material was taught can

influence the student's performance on the test. Baldwin and Howard (1983) found that accountancy students who sat an examination in which the questions were arranged in the same order in which the material had been covered in the module performed better than students taking the same questions arranged in a random order. By contrast, Gruber (1987) argues for a 'recency effect' to explain findings of a study in which students who sat tests in which questions had been arranged in reverse order in which they were presented in the module (with the most recent coming first) performed better that those who took the same test with the questions ordered randomly or in the same sequence in which they were taught. Stout and Wygal (1994) found that test-item sequencing relative to the order in which topics were taught had little effect on the performance of accountancy students.

Randomising test items

When administering summative examinations, it may be desirable to randomise questions and/or options in order to reduce the likelihood of cheating between students who are sitting in close proximity. Some CBA software allows for the random generation of test questions and distracters. However, as mentioned in the previous section, this may have an impact on the difficulty of the test.

You may also wish to use random selection in combination with question banks, which are collections of questions normally on one subject. In some software packages, items can be chosen at random from question banks, thus allowing a unique subset of questions to be chosen for each assessment or student. This is particularly useful for formative testing and enables students to test themselves on the same topic repeatedly, but with variety in the questions.

Chapter 8

Beyond objective testing

This chapter considers developments in CAA which go beyond the format of objective test-style questions. Although the majority of CAA which takes place in higher education is in the form of objective tests, there is an increasing number of examples of CAA which do not rely on such methods. Among these are systems which assess computer programming skills, evaluate project work and simulate the assessment of fieldwork. Additionally, CAA-related activities are increasingly being explored alongside the use of virtual learning environments and computer-mediated communication. This chapter also addresses the electronic marking of essays and the potential use of gaming techniques for assessment.

Extending CAA: programming, reflection, multimedia and simulation

In many ways, CAA exams which use multiple-choice style questions are largely replicating paper-based testing approaches. That is, although they may go some way towards exploiting technology by including images and sound, automated marking and feedback, and remote access, the basic format of the question is one which borrows heavily from traditional examining. In such assessments, where the answer is predetermined, the student is still in a relatively passive position. He/she chooses an answer to a question but is not able to challenge or shape it in any way. However, work in certain areas of CAA is leading to the development of assessments that are more interactive and quite far removed from both conventional testing and multiple-choice CAA (Bennett, 1998). Rather than simply mediating the transfer from page to screen, in some instances, CAA is enabling new types of activities to be included in assessment practices.

One example of the extension of CAA is the electronic assessment of computer programming skills. A number of systems have been developed to score and provide feedback on student computer programs (Halstead, 1994; Benford *et al.*, 1992; Foxley *et al.*, 1999). The Daly and Waldron (2002) argue that there are difficulties with assessing programming abilities using written examinations, because, among other reasons, examiners are trying to simultaneously measure syntax and the ability to solve problems. To counter this, they have developed RoboProf, an assessment tool which presents students with online problems which require programming solutions. Once the student has designed the solution they submit it to RoboProf, which runs it and compares its output against an expected output. The student receives a score, the output of their program and the expected output. They then have an opportunity to resubmit. Ceilidh (Computer Environment For Interactive Learning In Diverse Habitats) is a long-standing and widely used programming assessment system that can analyse coursework in 15 different programming languages. It has recently been redesigned as Coursemaster, which also allows online submission and contains an automatic marking facility for coursework. Additionally, it assesses diagrams, provides model answers, checks for plagiarism and offers extensive feedback (Foxley *et al.*, 2001). This use of online systems to assess student programs is an example of CAA enabling an activity which is difficult, if not impossible, to recreate on paper. Additionally, given the subject area, these assessments are arguably more authentic than paper-based tests.

A quite different use of CAA is as a reflective tool. An early such example was THESYS, an expert system designed at Nottingham Trent University, which guided students through a self-assessment of their undergraduate projects. The package comprised 38 generic questions in four sections which covered understanding, effort, time management, originality, quality of work, writing up and layout. Students ranked themselves against opposing statements and were given feedback on the strengths and weaknesses as they had identified them. There also existed a supervisor's marking package, and evaluation indicated that there was no significant variation in students' and supervisors' assessments of projects. The principles operating behind such a system are not unlike the model answer approach described by Laurillard *et al.* (2000) (discussed in Chapter 5) in which students working with an online learning package use comparisons with exemplar texts to reflect upon their own responses.

Some of the most exciting work in CAA involves the incorporation of multimedia into assessments. Video, audio and interactive graphics can convey a huge range of information and are increasingly features of the knowledge base of many different disciplines from history to chemistry, from art and design to geology. The introduction of multimedia elements into assessment practices allows students to demonstrate that they can work with information from a wide and varied range of sources. Research led by Professor Don Mackenzie (University of Derby) in the TRIADS CAA system has foregrounded the capacity of CAA to use multimedia applications to construct questions which are not feasible with paper-based tests. Within the TRIADS system there are approximately 30 defined question types – and the flexibility of the system allows those writing tests to combine different features and types of questions to invent their own style of questions. The question formats involve a much higher degree of interactivity than standard objective testing CAA. The authoring system, although complex, is powerful and questions can include a variety of interactive features, up to the level of full multimedia simulations.

Significantly, the TRIADS system is able to assess processes and procedures (such as laboratory- or fieldwork-based analysis) by using a combination of sequencing, building, classification and drawing activities. For example, a series of sophisticated, multimedia questions is used to assess students' fieldwork skills in geology – typically a practical activity which can be detrimentally affected by logistics and weather. During actual fieldwork exercises, students are encouraged to take good notes which are then used for the assessment which takes place three weeks later. The questions initially test knowledge of basic principles and then move on to explore the relationships between geological features. Subsequent question screens require students to interpret images, identify particular features on the screen and also draw a specific orientation on the screen. A zoom facility allows students to examine features in a similar way in which they would in the field. Overall, the questions require students to be knowledgeable about a range of geological characteristics, to be able to apply their knowledge to a given context and to identify patterns, components and relationships (ie analysis). (For a fuller account of this example, see http://www.gees.ac.uk/essd/field.htm#MackenD, accessed January 2003, and Mackenzie, 1999.) Many of the TRIADS questions are thought to be capable of testing higher learning levels (such as application, analysis and synthesis). For more information about the project and available question types, see the TRIADS website at http://www.derby.ac.uk/assess/talk/quicdemo.html (accessed January 2003).

The MCP Hahnemann School of Medicine at Drexel University (US) has constructed online exercises which help to develop and assess medical students' and physicians' knowledge of ethics and their communication skills. The exercises include four case studies which involve streamed video, photographs, sound and text according to the computing and networking capabilities of users. The studies consist of case notes, expert advice and the opportunity to interview a patient on an ethical issue. 'Patients' (human actors with a script) respond (verbally or textually depending on set-up) to questions which are entered as text by students. The range of questions which can be dealt with by the system is fairly comprehensive, and students are politely asked to rephrase questions where necessary. Students ultimately have to make an ethical decision and are then provided with detailed feedback on their ethical approach and communication skills. Alternative approaches are suggested where appropriate. This type of CAA is intended to complement rather than replace face-to-face interactions and practical examinations in medical ethics. Its merit is that it allows students to increase their exposure to realistic case studies and to practise engaging with ethical and moral issues in a 'neutral' space (see http://griffin.mcphu.edu/MedEthEx/intro.html, accessed January 2003).

Finally, computers can be used to simulate conditions under which students would normally be unable to practise. Such work is already increasingly common in the area of computer-assisted learning. For example, medicine and veterinary science often require skills in which it may be unethical or impractical to practise or assess other than in a simulated environment. One such example, from the University of Glasgow's Veterinary School, involves the use of a virtual horse's ovaries with which students perfect their physical examination techniques before working with real animals (Brewster *et al.*, 2000). In addition to enabling students to develop certain veterinary abilities before encountering live horses, the computerised model also allows a number of diseases and conditions to be simulated which students would not normally experience during their training. It is easy to see how the incorporation of such simulation into assessment practices (particularly self-assessment) would be beneficial.

An example in which computerised simulation can be an integral part of the assessment practice is the examination of trainee anaesthesiologists at the University of Toronto, also discussed in Chapter 5. As above, there are a number of practical and ethical dilemmas that surround the assessment of anaesthesia care. First, it is difficult to standardise student learning and examination experiences when working with human patients. Secondly, patients cannot be put at risk by the actions of trainees. Cleave-Hogg *et al.* (2000) describe the development of a 'computer-simulated patient' which enables anaesthesia students to practise and be assessed in a regulated, 'realistic' and observable environment. Using the CAE Med-Link

Simulator System, students work with a computer-operated mannequin in an operating room setting. The physiological functions (heart rate, breathing, expulsion of carbon dioxide) are all variable and numerous scenarios can be programmed. Following the simulation, which can be videotaped and observed by experts, students consult with experts to receive feedback and marks (Cleave-Hogg *et al.*, 2000).

Bennett predicts that the real growth area of CAA will be virtual reality simulations: 'These simulations will model environments – science labs, field experiences – giving students a chance to learn and be assessed under conditions similar to those encountered by practitioners' (Bennett, 1998). As discussed above, in a number of disciplines, CAA simulation can actually provide a more realistic and safer experience than is possible through other methods of assessment.

Virtual learning environments (VLEs) and computer-mediated communication (CMC)

In the last two years, many institutions have adopted Virtual Learning Environments (VLEs) (including Blackboard, WebCT, Learnwise, Lotus Learning Space, and Top Class, among others) to support student learning. (For an overview of VLEs, see the JISC Technology Applications Programme report *A Framework for Pedagogical Evaluation of Virtual Learning Environments*, Britain and Liber, 2000.) The growth in the use of VLEs has increased the potential for lecturers to integrate CAA into online learning: details of assignments, examination timetables, regulations and sources of help and advice can all be made available for students through a VLE via the Internet or intranet. Email and bulletin boards can be used to notify or remind students of deadlines. The assessment options within VLEs are normally limited to three or four simple item types and are generally unsuitable for summative assessment. Additionally, the functionality of the question features is limited; often they are more appropriate for conducting online surveys. However, a number of VLE software developers are working on allowing the integration of specialist assessment packages through application programming interfaces which would increase the range of item types. Nonetheless, currently VLEs offer the opportunity to provide self-assessment questions which can be embedded within learning materials, allowing students to check their progress as they are working in the VLE. For example, at University College London, a course in Clinical Skills developed by Professor Jane Dacre contains assessment MCQs, an objective structured clinical examination preparation case study and a database of photographic images (accompanied by descriptions) of locomotor system conditions. The main text of the course also contains embedded audio and video clips designed to help students practise taking medical histories and making diagnoses (Dacre and Haq, 2002).

VLEs also offer the opportunity to distribute group and individual feedback to students. For example, a file containing comments addressed to an entire class can be linked to a discussion session in which students query and discuss the feedback and assignment. Feedback on assessed work can be emailed to individual students, inviting them to raise questions (by email, phone, in person) as appropriate. The online environment may well encourage some otherwise reticent students to express their thoughts and concerns. Additionally, as suggested in Chapter 2, VLEs can be used for peer review among students. In this model of assessment, students' writing is circulated for comment and student reviewers offer feedback. Computer networks enable the tracking of essays and reviews, all of which can be submitted and administered electronically. For case studies of two computer-based, peer-assisted review projects, see Robinson (1999). Furthermore, it is thought by some writing researchers that electronic submission of coursework may foster an orientation towards the process of writing rather than the product (ie the grade) by facilitating drafting, annotation and revision (Pennington, 1996).

Finally, VLEs provide space for students to develop and publish web-based documents and coursework. In terms of assessment, this potentially enables a number of 'mixed-mode'-online learning and assessment activities, such as the review and analysis of websites, the creation of hypertext essays, the joint production of online presentations, and the contribution (or construction) of course-specific electronic resources. Such work might entail the rethinking of assessment criteria to accommodate issues such as relevance and authoritativeness of source material, multimodality, construction of non-linear arguments, coherence of presentation, awareness of audience, online functionality etc. Additionally, these online assignments might require a certain level of electronic literacy before students are able to participate (see Chapter 2).

Computer-mediated communication (CMC)

Participation in a VLE is likely to include discussion forums, often in the shape of online seminars, in which students engage in synchronous and asynchronous text exchanges with other students. There is increasing interest in exploring ways in which these interactions can be incorporated into assessment practices. Such approaches vary from assigning a small amount of credit for 'engaging' at any level, to the use of tools which graphically display levels of participation against defined criteria (Kuminek and Pilkington, 2001), to attempts to assess the value of individual's contributions. (Clearly the mere quantity of a student's participation in a seminar or discussion forum is no measure of the quality of their contribution.) In terms of the last suggestion, the electronic seminar has a key advantage over face-to-face sessions in that its narrative is preserved. This permits students to return to a discussion and reassess their contribution to it, tracing their role in the interplay of argument and counter-argument. These contributions can also be assessed by the module tutor and may figure in the overall mark.

Lea (2001) describes ways in which elements of online discourse generated during computer conferencing sessions were incorporated into assessment practices in an Open University course, H802, 'Applications of Information Technology in Open and Distance Education'. The assessment of online writing featured in two ways:

1   30 per cent of student marks were allocated based on the quality of contributions to online discussions.
2   Within the 2000-word required essay, students were asked to refer to five or more messages from the online debate and to comment on 'key points' made during the online conferences (Lea, 2001).

She argues that the use of online conferencing extends the 'rhetorical resources' available to students when developing arguments in course assessments. She also suggests that there is an increased reflexivity in the learning experience, comparable to that observed in studies with learning journals (Creme, 2000), because students are able to mull over and return to contributions (posted on the online message board) from their peers, a process largely absent from traditional teaching. Particular practices which Lea argues indicate a reflexive approach to learning (and writing) include 'leaving a time lag between reading and responding; making meaning in their writing through other students' messages; investing authority in others' messages in written assignments; [and] incorporating messages into written assignments' (Lea, 2001). Finally, she suggests that asking students to interweave CMC discourse into their essay assessment enables them to contemplate and acknowledge the collaborative writing process that online conferencing enables.

Automated marking of essays

Another way in which CAA may move beyond objective testing is through the computerised assessment of free text responses, a growing, but still relatively small area of CAA research. Chung and O'Neill (1997) provide a detailed overview of two main areas of work in computerised scoring of free text: project essay grade (PEG) and latent semantic analysis (LSA). PEG, an ongoing project begun by Ellis Page in the mid-1960s, relies on surface attributes (known as 'proxy variables') such as the rate of occurrence of uncommon words, use of prepositions and word count, all of which have been shown to be strong indicators of essay scores, as determined by human markers (Page and Peterson, 1995; Chung and O'Neill, 1997). Latent semantic analysis (LSA), initially devised for the purpose of information retrieval (Chung and O'Neill, 1997), uses statistical modelling to compare semantic similarity between texts to generate scores. It is based on the assumption that there is an 'underlying or latent structure' of word usage within an essay, and that this can be statistically measured and analysed (Foltz, 1996).

Chung and O'Neill cite studies which show that the level of agreement between the LSA system and a human marker is just slightly lower than the correlation between human markers. They suggest that while the PEG system is currently a better indicator of essay scores (with levels of agreement between the system and a human marker being equal to or higher than those between two human markers), LSA techniques have more potential for aiding the assessment of a wide range of activities including short-answer responses, text generated through computer conferencing and verbal exchanges.

One of the most prolific research centres in this area is the Natural Language Processing Group (NLPG) at the Educational Testing Service in Princeton. The NLPG work is also based on the use of LSA techniques to score free text responses. Much of their output describes the development and evaluation of the e-rater system, designed to score essays on a six-point scale according to syntax, argument structure and content (Burstein and Chodorow, 1999; Burstein, et al., 1996; Burstein, et al. 1998). A recent study based on 270 essays has shown that the correlation between the e-rater and a human marker was 0.73, compared with a correlation between two human markers of 0.75 (Burstein and Macru, 1999). However, in order to achieve high rates of accuracy, the e-rater system requires an 'optimal training set' of approximately 265 sample essays already scored by two people before it can 'mark' papers independently (Burstein et al., 2001). Although research is being done to reduce this sample size, the system is really designed to support large-scale essay examinations, such as the US Graduate Management Admissions Test, for which it has been used since 1999 to assess 750 000 essays (Burstein *et al.*, 2001). An additional drawback is the system's inability to give detailed, dialogic feedback on written work, although it should be noted that work on the development of grammatical and structural feedback is ongoing (Burstein *et al.*, 2001).

Gaming and assessment

In the last three years, there has been increasing interest in the use of video games and gaming techniques for learning and teaching. Games are available in various formats, such as through television (digital, satellite or with games console), computers, arcade consoles, portable games consoles and handheld electronic devices (eg phones, personal digital assistants). Most games involve simulations of one form or another, and the power and complexity of games has steadily increased. In the UK, the industry now has a turnover of £300 million per annum (DTI, 2001).

There is little research on why games are so popular. In 1981, Malone concluded that fantasy, challenge and curiosity were key motivators for repeated game playing. Research and development related to learning is usually focused on compulsory education. A study by the British Educational Communications and Technology Agency (2001) explored six computer games to support elements of the National Curriculum. A number of positive, if predictable, outcomes were identified which related to the importance of the role of the teacher and context of the game, increased motivation and collaboration, and the advantages of providing immediate feedback on actions and decisions. Other studies indicate benefits such as improved hand–eye coordination, the development of strategic, social, communication and sharing skills, stimulation of curiosity and familiarity with technologies (Kirriemuir, 2002a). A high level of collaboration, risk-taking and investment would appear to be required to produce successful educational games, of which there are few examples.

However, as Kirriemuir suggests, the qualities of existing games are relevant to a number of academic subjects:

> For example, geography and urban planning are associated with in-game landscape, building and community recreation; engineering and physics are essential to the realistic simulation of vehicles; history is useful for accurate recreations of events, characters and societies; the arts for character development; and music for sound effects (Kirriemuir, 2002b).

But it is also clear that 'what we learn from the few available studies is far from being comprehensive enough to provide us with a list of successful design features for good educational games' (Kafai, 2001). The use of games and gaming techniques offers particular advantages in extending the boundaries and capabilities of both learning and assessment. If, as current thinking and research indicates, games will increasingly be utilised to enhance and support student learning, then the impact on assessment methods and strategies should also be considered. The potential surely must exist to exploit gaming technologies for the benefit of assessing a range of generic and subject-specific skills, abilities and knowledge. The challenge would appear to be ensuring that assessment is not once again an afterthought in the process of curriculum development.

Chapter 9

CAA technologies

This chapter broadly considers the different types of technology which can be used for CAA. Due to the rapid pace of technological change, this chapter does not attempt to review particular software and systems. Rather, it provides an overview of CAA delivery methods including optically captured CAA (OMR, OCR, ICR) and screen-based CAA (computer- and web-based). The chapter also addresses related issues such as security, interoperability and standards. The authors would like to acknowledge the contribution of Myles Danson, CAA Manager, Loughborough University, to the section on optical data capture and Appendix B.

Optical data capture

Optical data-capture systems may include one, or a number, of the following technologies:

* *optical mark reading (OMR)*   automated capture of marks made on specially designed forms
* *optical character recognition (OCR)*   machine-rendered character reading (for example, scanning printed pages)
* *intelligent character reading (ICR)*   handwriting or machine print recognition
* *bar code*   a machine-readable bar code.

OMR entails the automatic reading and rudimentary analysis of information recorded on preprinted forms, thus eliminating the need for manual data entry. The technology has been used in marking multiple-choice questions since the 1950s, so is by no means new. OCR and ICR systems function similarly, but use a high specification optical scanner rather than a mark reader. This section focuses on OMR technology, but the majority

Table 9.1 Differences between OMR/OCR/ICR and stand-alone OMR
technology

Combined OMR/OCR/ICR	Stand-alone OMR
Scanner Auto-fed scanner throughput rates are in the region of 27 scripts per minute.	**Scanner** Auto-fed scanner throughput rates are in the region of 120 scripts per minute.
Stationery Can be laser printed black and white, systems have a high tolerance for damaged forms.	**Stationery** Requires high quality printing by a commercial printer and requires colour. Systems have a low tolerance for damaged forms.
Form design Supports a variety of input types including marks and handwriting. Form design software is relatively easy to use, is quick to produce a form from scratch, and is accessible to clients.	**Form design** Supports only mark reading. Form design software is less easy to use and may not be accessible to clients.
Archiving Forms or areas of forms are scanned and stored as image files, offering the opportunity for digital archiving.	**Archiving** The forms themselves should be archived as hard copy.

of processes described also apply to OCR and ICR systems (and combinations of these). Reference is given in the text where differences occur, and Table 9.1 provides a summary of the chief differences and the features of the technologies. Optically-captured results may be exported directly to existing databases or to statistical analysis packages. Item analysis is supported, allowing the improvement of question and test design over time. Candidate authentication may also be automated by using a unique identifier such as a student identification (ID) number, obviating the need for (potentially error-ridden) manual name entry and the problem of multiple records of common candidate names. Recent optical scanning software allows the support of some of the enhanced objective question formats described elsewhere; however, compared to other CAA techniques, fewer question types are available. Furthermore, where other CAA systems allow the inclusion of extensive feedback, an optical system is limited to reports on candidate performance. Results are not available instantaneously, but an optical CAA system can provide results within a very short time of the scripts being collated. Optical data capture is ideal for rapid and accurate scoring of simple multiple-choice questions, particularly in situations where assessing a group of students in a computer lab is impractical.

Methodology

Each candidate is supplied with a preprinted answer form. In the case of OMR, the correct answer is selected by scoring a mark through a predefined area on the form. ICR and OCR require the user to indicate responses within predefined, machine-readable areas on the form. The answer form may contain both the questions and areas for answers or just the answer area. If questions are included, then a unique form design and printing procedure must be undertaken for each assessment. This process ensures that the questions are not released to students and thus the questions can be reused in subsequent assessments. Intricate form design can allow imaginative and rigorous testing but is costly in terms of preparation and printing time.

If OMR assessment is being offered as a widespread service to academic staff, a generic answer sheet may be more supportable and scaleable. However, such a generic approach means that question format options are limited because they must conform to the answer sheet design.

The completed forms are collected after the assessment and taken for scanning and processing. The presence of a mark or character is detected by measuring the intensity and pattern of reflected light. This pattern of marks is translated into a data file and analysed using specialist software on a local computer. Results may be archived, if required, and can be linked to a central student records database. Question and test performance may also be examined using the resulting data.

In addition to standard scoring and analysis, many optical data-capture systems offer some or all of the following features:

- *Internet interface*   Once designed, forms can be printed as paper or converted to portable document format (PDF) or hypertext markup language (HTML), completed online and returned electronically for processing, or printed off and posted back for scanning. Fax capability can also be included.
- *Dictionary and database look-up*   A link to an external database enables the completion of partial records, such as the construction of a full address from just postcode and house number entries. This capability also helps to avoid the creation of duplicate records.
- *Multi-user option*   Multiple users can access desktop, form-design software.
- *Exporting data features*.
- *Reporting*   Automatically produced reports of various formats (see below for further detail on possible report formats).

- *Form conversion*   Existing paper forms can be scanned and set up for optical data capture (eg. from a word processed file).

Implementation options

Due to the initial outlay costs for optical data-capture CAA, it is most likely that it will be implemented at department, faculty or institutional level. Table 9.2 describes three different approaches to this form of CAA, all of which entail pre-test (form design and reproduction) and post-test (translation of the captured data to meaningful reports and spreadsheets) processing.

Key questions

The approach adopted is dependent upon a variety of factors, including financial resources, assessment load and available staff. In addition, it is prudent to consider the following questions:

- Will the hardware supplier allow trade-in of a hand-fed scanner for an automatic model at a later date?
- Is leasing rather than buying the scanner a better option?
- If a bureau does your processing, who keeps the archives of forms and results? Will a turnaround time of five to six working days suit academic schedules?
- How much manual data entry (eg student evaluations, research questionnaires) is currently taking place that could be transferred to an optical system if one were available?

Reports

Chapter 6 details some general approaches to the reporting and analysis of student results. The following are examples of report formats that can be generated by optical CAA systems:

- *Student results by student number*   This is a simple report giving the full test details of module code, test number, marking schedule, numbers of papers received and processed and the test date and processing date. There are gaps for the lecturer to fill in a module title and test title if desired. The report, which identifies results by student number, is anonymous and may be placed directly onto a notice board for dissemination.

Table 9.2 Optical data-capture technologies for CAA

<table>
<tr><td>

1 In-house hand-fed scanner

This is the least expensive hardware option, but is also the slowest to operate. Hand-fed scanners may give more control over the processing of forms that would be rejected as unreadable by automatic feeders. However, the increased processing time means that this option is probably better-suited to use at a departmental level rather than at an institutional level where volumes and frequency of use would be much greater.

---

2 In-house automatically-fed scanner

Auto-fed scanners offer higher throughput rates and (potentially) the ability to read double-sided forms. These are more expensive than hand-fed machines but they can cope with large-scale, institution-wide usage. Location of the equipment should take account of environmental conditions, and trained staff, skilled in error trapping, may be required for the processing stage.

---

3 External data-capture bureau service

A data-capture bureau can handle all aspects of this type of CAA, including the design and printing of stationery to guaranteed tolerances of reading. Tolerances of reading are important because if forms are poorly designed or ineffectively scanned, the reading of marks or characters may not be accurate. Once the assessment has been taken, the forms must be prepared and dispatched for processing by the bureau. This should involve a manual in-house check of students' marking of answers as well as the batching of forms according to student cohort or examination. In-house procedures to address the possibility of scripts being lost in transit (such as the precautionary scanning of forms to image files) should also be considered – especially for summative CAA. Forward bookings must be made with both the bureau and courier. The bureau will offer a maximum turnaround period (usually 3 working days) before forms, reports and electronic data are returned. Upon return, an in-house error check should be made before batching and dispatching results to staff and, subsequently, students. Generally, a bureau service is far less flexible than an in-house service. However, this should be offset by the advantage of not needing to invest in expensive hardware and maintenance contracts. For very large scale testing (such as standard medical exams) it may be advantageous to bring the bureau service on-site for processing.

</td></tr>
</table>

- *Student results in alphabetical order*   This report provides details of student names, ID numbers and results as percentages ordered alphabetically according to surname. The report can be used for investigating any individual student's results and performance.

- *Student results ranked from lowest to highest* Full test details along with results as percentages, candidate name and student number. This report is useful to check the spread of results. Weakest candidates are listed first.
- *Student results in order of processing* Useful for the test administrator to locate any answer forms without the student number completed correctly. These scripts will have been marked but no identity assigned.
- *Full results report* This report gives full test details along with a list of individual responses ordered by candidate number and programme code. The report allows trends in candidate answers to be identified quickly, and common errors which may be attributed to a lack of student knowledge, misunderstanding, or poor question design are readily apparent. Results are also listed by *programme code* with number of students, maximum score, minimum score, mean and standard deviation. This allows a comparison of programme performance for a particular module.
- *Question analysis and test summary report* The question analysis records for each question in the test:

  - the correct response (A–E)
  - the percentage of students choosing 'A', 'B', 'C', 'D', 'E'
  - the percentage of students answering correctly
  - the percentage of students answering incorrectly
  - the percentage of students selecting no answer
  - the percentage of students selecting more than one answer.

Protocols and procedures

As with all assessment, procedures should be put in place to ensure that quality is maintained. The introduction of technology into assessment practices often results in a re-evaluation and amendment of existing procedures and policies, particularly once the scale of operation of CAA has increased to departmental or faculty level. Appendix B provides examples of Codes of Practice and associated Service Level Statements for OMR CAA examinations. As discussed above, the *in-house* approach requires hardware, software and personnel on site, while the *bureau service* scans forms and produces reports remotely. The codes of practice for the two approaches are fairly similar (note the five-day turnaround for bureau); however, there are significant differences in the service level statements. (See Appendix B for a further discussion of scalability.)

Screen-based assessment

Screen-based assessment allows a wider range of question types than OMR, and, as suggested in Chapter 4, the technology can accommodate questions which use photographic images, audio, video and simulations. Unlike OMR, exercises can be interactive, adaptive and integrated into online learning software and environments. Automatic feedback (for correct and incorrect responses) is also possible and students can be provided with hints to aid them in reaching the correct answer. Like OMR, the scoring of many question types is automated, as is the generation of reports that analyse student and question performance.

There are a number of commercially produced CAA software systems, which usually comprise the following components:

- question authoring environment
- question management and administration
- question delivery environment
- reporting and analysis tools.

Although the basic structure of CAA software is similar, different packages offer different features and careful evaluation prior to purchase is encouraged. Increasingly, commercially produced software can be used to deliver stand-alone, closed network/intranet or web-based CAA. In addition, a number of CAA tools and environments have been developed within educational institutions, ranging from simple web-based, self-assessment programs to highly sophisticated and interactive assessment systems.

When selecting CAA software, there is a wide range of issues to consider, including pedagogical suitability of the software, interoperability, support costs, maintenance and upgrade contracts, licence fees and future development plans. Chapter 11 discusses the evaluation of software in greater detail.

Screen-based CAA uses software and networks to deliver assessments through one or more of the following mechanisms:

- stand-alone delivery on individual workstations;
- closed computer network/intranet (local, wide or metropolitan) delivery where one or more servers are used to present assessments to designated computers usually located on institutional sites;
- Internet technologies which deliver assessment through standard or proprietary web browsers which can be closed and secure, or open.

Stand-alone delivery involves assessments which are created using software and installed on an individual computer – either directly to the hard drive, or running from a CD ROM, disk or digital video disc. Answers may be saved within the software and can be downloaded manually.

A *closed computer network or intranet* consists of a set of machines linked to one or more servers and offers a more secure and versatile environment in which to deliver assessments. Questions are delivered to students across the closed network/intranet and their answer files are then stored on a server (rather than the hard drive of an individual machine). Typically, CAA software used on closed networks is coded and compiled, leading to high development costs. Such systems are usually operating system-specific; therefore, they tend to work well in enclosed environments. An intranet acts as a closed network but uses web technologies.

Web-based assessments are delivered across the Internet or on a local intranet, with the questions and answers residing on one or more central servers. A particular strength of Internet-delivered CAA is the potential flexibility of access that it offers, which can be advantageous for distance-learners and part-time students. As long as students have use of the Internet, they can take assessments at their own convenience.

As indicated earlier, the technologies used for CAA do not fall easily into definable categories; it is possible, and often desirable, to combine the use of two or more of the technologies outlined above. Figure 9.1 provides a generic overview and some exemplars for use of CAA. It is in no way definitive as there are many possible approaches to implementing the technology depending on purpose and resources.

As indicated in Figure 9.1, technologies can be used in combination for different types of assessment. For example, stand-alone delivery is usually used to provide self-assessment, because there is often less control over the testing environment and answers are not automatically transferred back to teaching staff. However, it is possible to develop stand-alone systems which are set up to allow secure summative assessment by collecting results from each computer manually, or to provide a partially stand-alone solution which, upon completion of the test, connects to a server or the Internet and transfers the results.

Closed networks are typically used for high-risk, summative CAA because they provide a secure and controllable environment, whereas, as suggested above, web-based assessments offer particular advantages for providing flexible assessments which may be accessed by both on- and off-campus students. In parallel with the increased use of the Internet generally, web-based assessment is one of the fastest growing areas of CAA. In terms of question content and format, these assessments can usually include all the

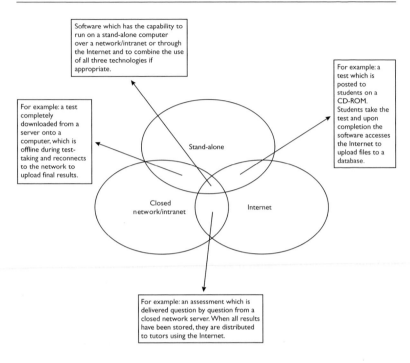

Software which has the capability to run on a stand-alone computer over a network/intranet or through the Internet and to combine the use of all three technologies if appropriate.

For example: a test which is posted to students on a CD-ROM. Students take the test and upon completion the software accesses the Internet to upload files to a database.

For example: a test completely downloaded from a server onto a computer, which is offline during test-taking and reconnects to the network to upload final results.

Stand-alone

Closed network/intranet

Internet

For example: an assessment which is delivered question by question from a closed network server. When all results have been stored, they are distributed to tutors using the Internet.

Figure 9.1 Overview of CAA technologies

graphical, audio and video material that up-to-date web browsers can support, but some specialist functions, such as mathematical symbols and specific language characters, can be difficult to display and enter in response to a question. The implementation of World Wide Web Consortium (W3C) standards enables cross-platform delivery, so theoretically, whatever the platform, all content is presented and functions in the same way. However, in practice, browser compatibility is still problematic due to the differing functionality and adherence to web standards of the two main web browsers. Interestingly, several CAA software systems provide their own proprietary browsers to overcome such delivery issues and provide a secure testing environment. Within a closed network or intranet, a specially defined browser can be installed and its features controlled, which can help minimise presentation and functionality problems. Despite these difficulties, web technology is constantly being developed, unlike some other older technologies, and holds much future potential for CAA.

The mechanics of delivering online assessments also feature prominently in screen-based CAA. Although the Internet offers the advantage of remote delivery over closed networks, this approach is reliant on many Internet links that cannot be guaranteed. The quality of web-based CAA can also be degraded by Internet traffic, which, again, is out of the control of institutions. For a closed network delivery of CAA across geographically dispersed sites, an institution would need to invest in hardware links between the sites, or rely on the facilities of a telecommunications provider which may vary from one location to another. For both closed network and web-based CAA, bandwidth can limit test design. For example, low bandwidth may restrict the number of graphics which can be simultaneously delivered to large numbers of students. For all types of delivery, consideration needs to be given to what other computing resources students can access during the test. For example, should they be able to use stored files, email, search engines or chat groups during assessments? Do they need to use certain software tools such as spreadsheets or databases? Some software can provide a bespoke and secure environment for test-taking which enables access only to resources necessary for completion of the assessment.

Security

Security presents a particular challenge to CAA and it is often presumed that security issues should be resolved technologically. Although there are some questions of security that are particular to the way in which software stores and delivers assessments, there are also many operational security issues which apply to summative assessment generally. It is important to remember that there are usually policies in place for dealing with issues such as academic misconduct and plagiarism which can be equally applied to CAA.

For some, the holy grail of CAA is the off-campus delivery of summative assessment. This clearly presents challenges in terms of the authentication of the student. However, exactly the same challenges would be faced if remote, non-invigilated, paper-based assessment were attempted. Current software systems do provide some mechanisms for authentication, including the issuing of passwords and 'access tokens' to allow students to take assessments at scheduled times. These go some way towards assuring that the person who accesses and takes a test is who they say they are. However, without either physical or remote invigilation (using, for example, omni-directional webcams), it is not possible to ensure that students are not colluding, consulting textbooks or accessing information through other means. It is, perhaps, worth noting that existing mechanisms for authenticating paper-based summative assessments are often minimal, sometimes not even requiring photo identification.

Biometric identification and verification technologies are increasingly used for financial transactions and personal data privacy. Technologies in current use and under development include face, hand and finger geometry, handwriting, iris, vein patterns and voice recognition (Biometric Consortium, 2002). Current use of such technologies in education is limited – examples include a Philadelphia School System which uses finger printing technology to track teachers (Borga, 2002) – but as costs decline and greater integration of technologies is achieved, it is likely that biometrics will play a role in authenticating students for distance summative examinations. Again, however, a fingerprint authentication at the beginning of a remote examination would not assure that that student continued to take the examination.

To date, there has not been extensive use of CAA to deliver distance summative assessments. Security of questions and answers within software is particularly important if CAA is to be used for summative and high stakes assessment. Encryption is a standard mechanism for ensuring that questions and answers can not be accessed and CAA software for summative assessment should be implemented with a minimum of 128-bit industry-standard encryption of question and answer files. Web-based assessment is less secure in terms of the actual transfer of files than closed network delivery because the files could, in theory, be intercepted en route between the client and user machines. The fewer possible routes for the data to travel, the less likely the chances of interception. However, if files are encrypted, the information within is still potentially protected from the interceptor. A Virtual Private Network (VPN) makes it possible to run a web-based, closed network and is one possible mechanism for ensuring that secure assessments can be delivered over the Internet (see MacDonald (2002) for an overview of VPNs).

Interoperability

Interoperability describes the capacity for different systems to share information and services such that two or more networks can communicate with each other to exchange data in a common file format. For example, mobile phone networks operate on different systems, yet exchange data in such a way that it is possible to use a phone on one network to communicate with someone on a phone on another network. Interoperability is important to prevent 'vendor lock-in'. In terms of CAA, you might invest in a particular assessment system, create several thousand questions, and after four years decide to move to another system which offers more desirable features. If the original system is not interoperable (that is, it does not 'talk' to any other systems), it is likely that the questions you have created will be locked into the system and will have to be transported manually into the new CAA system.

Extensible Markup Language (XML) has been defined by the W3C as the technology upon which interoperability should be based. XML is unlike other mark-up languages such as HTML, where 'tags' are predefined. (Tags are sequences of characters that both 'define' chunks of information and 'describe' how that information should look when displayed or printed.) XML, in contrast, supports user-defined tags, which makes it a highly flexible and powerful technology. However, this flexibility sets up a certain tension. On the one hand, it means that anyone can define an unlimited number of tags, while on the other hand, for systems to interoperate they need to share a common set of tags. Thus, in order for tags to be understood across assessment systems, some standards must be defined and adhered to.

Standards

The IMS (Instructional Management Systems) Global Learning Consortium is the most advanced of the standards bodies. Originally formed in 1997 as an Educom project, its membership is extensive, including nearly all learning software developers, publishers, Microsoft™, the W3C, Joint Information Systems Committee (JISC), the British Educational Communications and Technology Agency, University for Industry and the US Department of Defence. In the UK, the Centre for Educational Technology Interoperability Standards is funded by JISC to represent higher and further education in various standards initiatives including IMS.

Standards are becoming increasingly important. Most of the major vendors of virtual learning environments (VLEs) are working towards IMS and SCORM standards compliance. (SCORM stands for 'Shareable Content Object Reference Model', was developed by ADLnet, and is closely aligned with IMS standards.) The danger with a multitude of standards is that the strength of the standard is determined by uptake, which, within the context of rapidly evolving technology, can be difficult to achieve. Standards also signal a possible point of conflict between conformance, on the one hand, which potentially facilitates the sharing and transfer of questions and other information, and creativity and capacity for unconstrained question and software development on the other.

The issues surrounding the definition of standards, uptake and compliance are complex. Users' and suppliers' needs are different: the cost associated with adopting standards is significant for suppliers, while users would like broad and well-defined standards. To define standards, common vocabulary and definitions for terminology must be agreed by a wide variety of users from educational, training and business sectors, research organisations, software and systems developers, and other organisations and initiatives (such as international standards organisations). There is a range of standards currently under development to cover metadata, content, enterprise, learner information, question and test, accessibility, learning design, collaboration and user requirements.

The IMS Question and Test Interoperability (QTI) specification has been under development for a number of years, and although not yet an international standard, it seems to have achieved enough stability for vendors of CAA software to have developed systems which allow the exchange of questions. While this is encouraging, a recent evaluation of the tools developed by vendors to meet the specification indicates that only the simplest of question types are currently achievable with ease (Sclater et al., 2002). As well as the QTI specification, the Enterprise specification may also be relevant to CAA, especially where integration with management information systems is sought in order to transfer relevant student information and marks.

Standards potentially offer benefits to those who wish to use CAA, by enhancing the opportunities for sharing and exchanging questions, thus eliminating the need to replicate questions in new assessment environments. There is some way to go, however, before the potential is realised.

Sector collaboration

One of the most time-consuming aspects of CAA is the construction and evaluation of test questions. As suggested elsewhere, good questions can be difficult to write, even for an experienced writer. Significant gains could be made if discipline-based collaboration were undertaken across the sector so that academics from different institutions could share and reuse good material. Ideally, such a collaboration would be well-placed to receive pedagogic and technical support from discipline-based national bodies.

Bull and Dalziel (2003) explore the issues of re-using questions, which can be a straightforward exchange and re-use of questions in their original format, or may take the form of sharing questions to help inspire and inform development of further questions, modification of questions to create new resources or the re-purposing of questions to meet previously unidentified needs. Key issues which emerge are the need for standards to be adequately defined and widely adopted and appropriate models for copyright, intellectual property rights and digital rights management.

Chapter 10

Operational, technical and support issues

This chapter outlines a range of operational and technical issues associated with summative CAA, including software evaluation, installation and maintenance, risk analysis, security, timetabling, contingency plans, plagiarism and staff development. Most of the procedures described below apply specifically to screen-based assessment, rather than the use of optical CAA systems, which tend to have more in common procedurally with paper-based examinations. However, further details on the operational aspects of optical CAA systems are provided in Chapter 9 and Appendix B. Despite the emphasis in this chapter on summative CAA, which is by nature a more rigorous activity than formative assessment, many of the same processes can be adopted to aid the smooth running of all CAA.

Evaluation and integration of software

Identifying the appropriate software for a CAA system is a crucial early decision, which should be undertaken by a committee of staff including representatives from academic departments, computer services, the learning technology/CAA unit (or equivalent), students and educational developers. It may be useful to speak with staff in other departments or institutions who are already using the software in order to learn more about its strengths and weaknesses. Software and systems should be evaluated in terms of:

- pedagogic suitability
- internal robustness
- ease of use
- accessibility
- interoperability with other computerised systems
- flexibility and portability
- ease of distribution, installation and maintenance.

It is clearly important that the tools chosen are compatible with the available network and desktop operating systems and any auxiliary software that test designers may wish to use concurrently during an assessment, such as an electronic calculator, audio/video players and word processing facilities. If possible, contact the software developers to see if they will allow access to the programme's code or provide some kind of application programming interface to enable a more detailed exploration of the software structure and flexibility in customisation.

It is also wise to consider the level of technical support and maintenance provided with the software. Commercial packages may be more expensive than those developed as a result of HE-funded initiatives, but may also be better supported and have a longer shelf life. Alternatively, software derived from educational research projects may allow greater flexibility, open source coding and potential for tailoring to institutional needs.

To guide the evaluation process (particularly in terms of educational qualities of the technology), a toolkit such as the one proposed in Oliver and Conole (1998) may be useful.

Evaluating the integrity and reliability of systems

With OMR technology there is no risk of technological failure jeopardising the sitting of an examination, as the technology is not used until after the examination has taken place. However, running summative examinations using screen-based assessment can be a high-risk activity. Therefore, it is worth considering the following suggestions when assessing the suitability of your computer system for delivering screen-based assessment:

- Use more than one server to deliver the test. For example, consider spreading the test load across two or more servers. If one server fails, only some of the students will be affected and, if necessary, this group can be moved onto the servers which are still functioning. This strategy only works effectively if back-up systems are already in place and transference can be performed rapidly.
- Ensure that a reliable, internal back-up system is in place for answer files.
- Network cards, infrastructure and servers, and client machines should be fast enough to prevent bottlenecks from forming. As a specific example, network cards should be probably be running at 100 Base T or above, though the required speed depends on the type of system used.
- Restrict other computing activity on the servers and network segment during the examination period.

Depending on the scale of use, it might be worth setting up an independent system which is only for use with screen-based assessment and contains its own servers. One advantage of a separate system is that there are no other users or activities competing for space. Additionally, the use of dedicated servers makes it easier to restrict student access to other applications (such as the Internet or email) during assessments.

Identifying key individuals

CAA generally involves disparate groups of staff within a university who may be responsible for areas such as examination questions and design, pedagogical and technical support, supervision of computer system(s) and quality assurance regulations. The identification of these individuals depends, in part, on the type and scale of CAA being implemented. If, for example, testing is largely for formative or self-assessment purposes and is contained within a department, then those involved will include academic authors of the assessments and, possibly, educational technologists, who might provide pedagogic and technical support. They can probably be found within the faculty or department, educational development unit and computer services. Generally, when CAA is used summatively (and as the use of CAA grows across the institution), a wider number and range of people are likely to be involved, including members of staff responsible for examinations, quality assurance, and learning and teaching. Large-scale implementation may dictate that a central CAA officer (or unit) is required to co-ordinate the varied groups involved in CAA. Additionally, if summative CAA becomes more broadly adopted, a university-wide strategy for online examinations may be valuable.

Risk analysis

If CAA is to be used for summative assessment, it is useful to conduct a risk analysis. The process of risk analysis can be used to help instil confidence in the resultant procedures of the CAA system(s). By consulting widely with students, academics, computing staff, educationalists, senior management etc, it may be possible to foster a sense of ownership in and support for the chosen approach(es).

In order to make the risk analysis as comprehensive as possible, try to anticipate potential risks from different perspectives. In particular, it is worth considering the following groups:

- students
- lecturers

Table 10.1   Example risks for different groups

Students

- Poor examination performance due to anxiety about or inexperience with computers
- Failure to record responses due to misunderstanding of technical procedures in examination

Teachings

- Loss of control of the assessment process
- Inability to ask appropriate questions due to lack of understanding of question types and/or limitations of software
- Loss of summative scores due to machine failure
- Invalidation of results due to a security breach

Senior managers

- Higher than expected initial costs (financial and time) of system
- Higher than expected maintenance costs
- Poor publicity for institution in the event of system failure during exams
- Resistance to CAA from teaching staff

Computing staff

- Computer or system failure
- Pressure on resources
- Inability to support specified software and hardware

- examinations staff
- administrative staff
- computer services staff
- senior managers
- quality assurance staff
- prospective employers

It is advisable to include representatives from any relevant groups in the consultation process discussed above. Table 10.1 provides an overview of samples of risks posed for different groups involved with CAA.

Once risks have been identified, the probability and consequences of such events should be evaluated so that plans can be developed to ensure that the implementation of CAA is as smooth as possible. Such planning would include designing courses for staff development, pre-examination day procedures, examination day protocols and contingency plans, post-exam security plans and checklists (see Appendix C).

Installing and maintaining software

Technical staff should be trained in how and where to install CAA software. They will need to understand the network configuration, relevant operating systems and the security protocols in order to install tests correctly. It is also advisable that they receive training on the way the software operates. Ideally, the same person(s) who installs and maintains the software should be present during the examination to oversee the technical side of the assessment and to respond to any problems which may arise. They should also be advised of techniques for testing the system in advance of the candidates' arrival.

Both technicians and academics (especially those involved with invigilation) should be made aware of all procedures several weeks before the assessment period. In particular, maintenance checks should be performed on hardware and software, and where problems arise, the necessary repairs should be made. If appropriate, this process should be undertaken in liaison with the department responsible for timetabling so that the necessary arrangements can be made. For example, if five machines are unusable in the CAA examination area, the office responsible for timetabling must be given this information in advance so that no students are assigned to these workstations.

Security

The security of question and answer files is paramount if CAA is being used for summative assessment. In order to minimise the risk of unauthorised access to these files, and depending on the level of security available on the overall system, it may be advisable to load question files onto the network shortly before the examination begins and to remove both the question and answer files from the server as soon as the assessment concludes. It is also important that any additional copies of the examination, for example on disk or paper, are kept secure. Prior to starting the assessment, students' identities should be verified, as with standard examinations.

During the test, if the CAA software allows, computing staff should check that the number of students taking the assessment tallies with the number of answer files being created on the server. This helps to ensure that all students are submitting answers properly and that the system is creating a separate file for every candidate.

Relevant members of staff in the computing, CAA, examinations and administrative units, should be made aware of all security procedures for the periods before, during and after the examinations. It is advised that security arrangements be distributed to all parties in writing, so that they are followed consistently across the institution.

Timetabling

From an operational perspective, the scheduling of CAA requires careful planning, particularly when being used for summative purposes. While OMR assessments can be timetabled for a standard examination room, screen-based assessment tests require computer laboratories that can accommodate the student cohort taking the assessment.

Those involved with timetabling examinations should be offered guidance in the additional requirements of CAA. Particular considerations might include pre-test equipment audits, hardware availability, computer lab capacity, and time required to load and download question/answer files and for student login. For screen-based assessments, it may be necessary to deliver successive sessions of the same examination where large numbers are involved and this typically requires greater planning and organisation than traditional examinations. In order to operate a successful screen-based assessment system, a sufficient number of PCs is required. Ideally, these will be networked machines situated in one or more computer laboratories or resource centres. The machines should be powerful enough to run the chosen software and they should be of a similar specification so that no students receive an unfair advantage due to the processing power of individual machines. When booking a computer laboratory, it is advisable to leave approximately ten per cent spare capacity, so that machines are available in the event of workstation failure.

The screen-based examination can be delivered in a single computer laboratory or in a number of laboratories which are timetabled simultaneously. If a large group of students cannot be accommodated in one sitting, a second group can take the exam immediately following the completion of the first group. The two groups must be kept separate at all times to prevent candidates from conferring (King *et al.*, 1998; Zakrzewski and Bull, 1998). Table 10.2 provides a case study of timetabling CAA examinations at the University of Luton.

If CAA is to be used on a medium or large scale, then the impact of such provision upon other computing resources must be evaluated. Both

Table 10.2   Timetabling CAA at the University of Luton

At Luton, a large computing laboratory was constructed as part of a new learning resource centre built in the mid-1990s. The facility is open year-round for students to access machines; however, it is closed throughout the two-week examination period at the end of every semester. During this period, it is treated like any other examinations space in the university and is timetabled accordingly.

The lab contains 185 machines and a typical examination schedule might look like the following:

9.00–10.00	Mathematics	A1000 – group 1
10.30–11.30	Mathematics	A1000 – group 2
12.00–13.00	Chemistry	B1100
13.30–14.30	Geography	A1300
15.00–16.00	Mathematics	C2000
18.00–19.00	Linguistics	B3300

It is recommended that a minimum of 30 minutes is left between examinations.

Allocation of resources and computing staff time during the examination period:

Since the Learning Resources computer suite is used exclusively for testing during the examinations period, students wishing to access computers for other activities (such as word processing assignments, email, Internet research) must use machines located in other areas of the Learning Resources Centre and those maintained in their faculties.

Approximately 30 computing staff hours are allocated to the pre-examination preparation period. Activities during this time would include installing sample tests on the network for student practice, clearing space on the server, if necessary, and checking and updating identification and security procedures. Additionally, all workstations are tested to ensure that they are operating correctly.

During the delivery of CAA examinations, one computing staff member is always present in the computer laboratory with others on standby. Computing staff are responsible for loading tests onto the network, saving and downloading answer files, monitoring student responses for cheating, and removing question and answer files.

A dedicated, smaller computing suite is reserved for students with special needs who may require modified workstations, additional software or extra time.

summative and formative CAA can affect students' access to other facilities such as email, Internet and computer conferencing, and a balance may need to be struck to ensure other online activities are not diminished.

Summative CAA may present the most significant complications in terms of managing computing resources. For example, if a computer laboratory is timetabled for CAA for the duration of an examination period, organisers should consider whether a sufficient number of machines and resources are available elsewhere in the institution for normal use. Organisers should also determine whether support staff will be overstretched by trying to manage the operation of CAA while continuing to maintain a service for other staff and students. The capacity of networks should also be evaluated: a period of high CAA activity may result in slower network speeds and have an impact on other activities taking place.

To address these and similar issues, it is useful to conduct a feasibility study (which incorporates a usage survey) during the planning stages for CAA. Additionally, appropriate support staff should collaborate to optimise the allocation of resources during these periods of high use.

Finally, the scheduling of formative CAA, though less critical, might also take into account a number of the above considerations such as timing, computer availability and network speed and capacity. It is important that for both summative and formative assessments, access issues are resolved so that all students have the same opportunity to take the assessments.

Back-up procedures

A common worry of those considering adopting CBA is computer failure – either of one or more workstations, a server or an entire system. Things can go wrong during screen-based assessment examinations, but if detailed back-up procedures are in place, staff can proceed confidently in the knowledge that students will still be fairly assessed.

Contingency arrangements

Clear guidelines should be provided to all participating staff so that they know how to respond in the event of one or more workstation failures. These should be available in written form, and everyone involved with the assessment should be briefed in advance. The guidelines should advise an invigilator on how to proceed after the failure of the machine(s). Depending on the number of machines affected and the extent to which the assessment has been completed, the invigilator might attempt to restart machines, transfer the students affected to new workstations, end the examination or provide paper copies of the examination (Zakzrewski and Bull, 1998; Heard *et al.*, 1997a). A brief report on workstation failures and other aberrations should be compiled following the session and it should be kept on file in case it is required by an examinations board. For detailed instructions to invigilators on the procedures to follow in case of computer failure(s), see Appendix C.

Systems and equipment provision

As suggested above, when scheduling screen-based assessment examinations, a certain percentage of workstations should be left empty, so that they can be used in the event of the failure of other individual machines. Rooms should also contain spare equipment for workstations, such as mice, keyboards and cables. Each workstation should have a set of written instructions and a page of common procedural errors and solutions for students to consult during the examination. Telephone facilities should also be available so that support and teaching staff can be contacted, if necessary.

Collation and transfer of results

Some screen-based software will automatically save each response given by a student to the server incrementally. Other software will only save answers once the student has completed all the questions and is finishing the test. For summative assessment, it is useful to have the answers saved as the student progresses through an examination so that should the system fail some results will be available. In cases where failure occurs late in the examination, it may be deemed that students have completed a sufficient amount of the assessment for an accurate mark of their achievement to be awarded.

Clear guidelines on the removal of answer files from the server and their transfer, storage and archiving should be made available to all those involved with the collation of results, including teaching and support staff, examinations office and departmental administrators.

Operational procedures

As with contingency plans, the presence of appropriate procedures for all stages, particularly leading up to and during CAA, instils confidence in the system. All those involved in the invigilation of CAA should be provided with training on test operational procedures, including logging in protocols, student identification, reading of instructions, timing and policy on when students can enter and leave the examination area. Additionally, as with traditional examinations, those staff members present during the CAA examination may need to know how to advise students who turn up late, find that they are in the wrong assessment, or suffer from severe stress. The British Standards Institute has produced a standard for the delivery of screen-based assessments. BS 7988 is a code of practice for the use of IT for the delivery of assessments. The code of practice has 17 sections, the majority of which are not influenced by the application of CAA software, and distinguishes between high and low stakes assessment. Three primary roles in the delivery of CAA are defined: assessment sponsors, distributors and assessment centres. The standard addresses the delivery, scoring, security, authenticity, validity, consistency and quality of CAA at an operational level (Grove-Stephenson *et al.*, 2002; British Standards Institution, 2002). Compliance with the standard is a considerable undertaking and may be particularly challenging for educational institutions where computers are used for multiple purposes.

Finally, it is wise to secure the room to be used for summative CAA in advance to allow final checks to be made on both hardware and software. This should include testing that the examination is operating correctly, (opening, displaying questions, saving answers etc) and that any additional software required is available. In order to cope with large numbers and to prevent collusion, it is useful to assign students to particular computers; this may involve numbering machines prior to the assessment.

At the start of the examination, procedures similar to those used for paper assessments will need to be followed to allow authentication of students. Verbal instructions should be given at this stage, and it may also be necessary for students to be provided with brief written instructions to which they can refer during the examination. Appendix C provides examples of such instructions. For a more detailed review of procedural issues in CAA examinations see Zakrzewski and Bull (1998).

Countering cheating

Opportunities for students to plagiarise during examinations should be minimised, and existing procedures and policies regarding plagiarism and examinations can be applied to CAA. However, the layout of computer laboratories designed for open access or teaching may result in workstations being located close together, providing the opportunity for students to view each others' screens. To counter this, privacy screens can be fitted around workstations to prevent students looking onto others' work (Zakrzewski and Bull, 1998). If multiple examinations are being delivered in the room, then students taking different examinations can be seated at alternate workstations to prevent copying.

Electronic means of combating cheating include randomising questions and monitoring student responses. Randomisation can take any of the following forms:

- The list of answer options for each question can be randomised.
- The order of questions can be randomised.
- The choice of test questions (selected from one or more question banks) can be generated at random, so that no two students will be taking an identical test. (To use this method, tutors must be certain of the validity and reliability of questions.)

In order to monitor student work during an assessment, some software products allow response files to be viewed during the examination as answers are submitted. If cheating is suspected, it can quickly be determined whether students positioned at adjacent workstations are simultaneously recording the same responses.

Security and transmission of results

At the end of the examination, results should be collated and stored on a disk/CD or in a protected and secure part of the server. Copies of the results and the question files can be stored with the appropriate support or teaching departments such as the examinations office, registry, department or CAA unit. The test can then be deleted from the server. If it is the policy to allow the re-use of questions and tests, no copies of the test should be released to students. Alternatively, it may be decided to make some or all of the past test questions available for revision purposes.

For further discussion of CAA procedures, see King *et al.* (1998); Zakrzewski and Bull (1998); Heard *et al.* (1997a) and King and White (1999).

Student support

It is essential that students are provided with appropriate support and training for CAA so that their performance is not diminished by fear of, or inexperience with, technology. For examinations, you may wish to prepare your students by providing computerised tests (as formative or self-assessment exercises) throughout the module. Additionally, the software and question types can be demonstrated to students during a lecture or workshop.

However, if students do not gain experience of working with CAA during the term, then support sessions must be made available to them prior to the CAA examination. Students may also be uncertain about revision strategies for the types of test questions that they will encounter in such a session.

Both the technology and the question types used in CAA may be new to students. Tutors should advise students of the new procedures well before any examination, and candidates should be given an opportunity to practise with questions and technology. Example questions – representative in content and format of the examination items – can be made available two to three weeks in advance of the examination and students can practise either on their own or in supported sessions.

Students should also be provided with a set of written instructions that explain the procedures of the examination and make clear what will happen if one or more workstations fail during the session. Above all else, technology should not get in the way of a student achieving a score that accurately reflects his or her ability.

Provision for students with special needs

Research is ongoing to develop guidelines for the design and delivery of CAA for students with disabilities including dyslexia, visual and hearing impairments and mobility problems. However, often students with special needs require support on an individual basis.

Disability and examinations offices are likely to have established practices concerning assessing students who are registered disabled. Wherever possible, the same practice should be followed with CAA. For example, if dyslexic students are allocated additional time in traditional exams, then the same should hold for CAA. Another possible approach is to adopt a policy which states that all students with special needs should be given the choice of taking the examination on computer or on paper. However, if this is the case, effort will have to be made to ensure that examinations designed for computer delivery translate easily to paper presentation. As CAA becomes increasingly sophisticated this may be problematic. (See also Chapter 6 for a discussion of the potential impact upon performance of different test formats.)

In the UK, the introduction of the Special Educational Needs and Disability Act (2001) poses some important questions about the development and use of computerised assessments. The requirement for electronic resources to be accessible covers drill and practice tests as well as formative and summative assessments.

As a starting point, colleagues may wish to investigate whether their computerised assessment materials can be used in conjunction with assistive technologies such as screen readers (text to speech converters) and magnifiers. Additionally, accessibility may be improved through the customising of an operating system's display settings and, where appropriate, Internet browser configurations. The special needs advisor at your institution may be able to offer suggestions on issues such as screen design, background colour, font size etc. Other groups that can provide information include TechDis (http://www.techdis.ac.uk), SKILL (http://www.skill.org.uk/) and the Trace Research and Development Centre (http://trace.wisc.edu/) (websites accessed January 2003).

Academic staff development

Opportunities for subject specialists to critically discuss and debate the potential of online assessment are crucial. Such opportunities might take the shape of educational development workshops, topics within a postgraduate programme in higher education (such as an MA in Academic Practice or a Certificate in Learning and Teaching), a discussion in a departmental teaching committee, a small research project, or an institution-wide seminar. An educational development approach might focus on the pedagogical implications of CAA, the design of questions and tests, and ways in which CAA would complement existing assessment methods. This approach might involve a series of workshops including an introductory session covering the following topics:

- overview of CAA – providing an understanding what CAA is and its potential for use by teaching staff
- current use in higher education – an account of current activity and case study examples to provide context
- accessibility issues
- available delivery mechanisms.

An introductory session could be followed up with fuller sessions which explore different aspects of CAA such as question and test design and allow participants to gain hands-on experience of working with online assessment. (Example programmes for half- and full-day staff development sessions are given in Appendix D.) Where objective tests are being used, further sessions might be held which explore with participants:

- the types of objective tests that can be developed
- the learning which can be assessed using them

- designing questions – both basic and more advanced question types
- designing feedback
- scoring
- use of appropriate technology
- analysing results and statistical reports
- test and question bank design and use.

It is advisable to introduce CAA within the context of adopting an appropriate assessment method which complements existing learning, teaching and assessment methods and strategies. Educational development should initially focus on the assessment rather than the delivery mechanism. However, to provide the correct context, it is likely that it will be necessary to demonstrate and/or provide a brief overview of the appropriate CAA delivery mechanism(s).

Where academics are not required to create tests using the software, but are assisted in this activity by support staff, familiarity with software and, where appropriate, hardware is still important. Introductory sessions should provide:

- an overview of the software or OMR question and response cards from the student perspective
- practical experience of the range of question types available
- guidance on writing questions which will appear on screen rather than on paper
- suggestions on question layout and style for the appropriate delivery mechanism
- an understanding of the role of central support services in the running of CAA.

If staff are expected to use software themselves to create tests, training and continuing support should be given in the use of the software.

Additionally, for summative assessment, knowledge and understanding of policies and procedures become critical to the success of the system. Staff should be given training in their responsibilities with regard to:

- *pre-examination procedures*   the process of preparing tests, administrative and quality assurance procedures, security, student support and training;
- *during examinations*   invigilation, back-up procedures and special circumstances;
- *post-examination procedures*   the collation and collection of results,

quality assurance procedures regarding analysis of reports, updating questions, security of results and feedback to students;
* documentation which supports the system;
* the role and duties of support and other staff involved in running the system.

Where only formative or self-assessment is taking place, it may not be necessary to run formal staff development sessions covering the operational aspects of CAA. Well-structured documentation and the identification of a key individual who coordinates CAA activity may be sufficient to guide staff through the process of setting and delivering tests.

Support staff development

We use the term 'support staff' to identify all those who may be involved in the implementation and evaluation of CAA who are not teaching staff or senior managers. This is likely to include a range of individuals and groups within a given institution, such as:

* librarians and learning resource specialists
* information and computer services staff, including those who support software, hardware and networks
* learning technologists
* educational developers
* administrators, located centrally and within faculties and departments
* quality assurance staff.

The composition of staff involved in the delivery of CAA will vary according to organisational structure and specific roles and responsibilities. For this reason, we have not attempted to detail the staff development issues for each of these groups, as their roles will vary between different institutions and possibly departments. Instead, we have identified the following major issues which need to be addressed for support staff in the delivery, maintenance and support of CAA:

* installing and maintaining software
* installing tests
* pre-test audits
* security of test and result information
* back-up procedures for system/equipment failure
* collation and transfer of results

- assisting and supporting students
- test operational procedures
- timetabling and computer allocation.

It is essential that all participating staff are offered the appropriate training and continued support in the preparation, delivery, administration and security of CAA. It is recommended that a series of pilot tests, which replicate test protocols, are carried out to guarantee that everyone involved with CAA is fully aware of the test procedures.

Managing the introduction of CAA at an institutional level

Getting started

The literature offers few structured institution-wide approaches to imple menting CAA. Stephens *et al.* (1998) and King (1997) provide some general protocols for introducing online assessment, and the former compares university-wide with departmentally organised CAA systems. One of the difficulties of introducing a new technology, particularly one as potentially contentious as CAA, is persuading colleagues and senior managers of the possible benefits. These might include learning enhancement, capacity to create assessments which are not possible on paper, and some educational and cost efficiencies (particularly in terms of savings in marking time).

In order to stimulate a discussion of CAA and demonstrate its capabilities, it can be valuable to:

- Identify and analyse case studies from other institutions and consider how such models might be modified to work in your organisation.
- Obtain sample copies of software to conduct demonstrations.
- Find examples of good test questions in order to illustrate the pedagogical fitness for the purpose of the assessment methods.
- Identify the key inhibitors and drivers for your institution and try to learn and understand both their implicit and explicit priorities.
- Determine where CAA might be positioned within an institution's key strategies and policies. For example, if widening participation is a part of your institution's medium-term strategy, then perhaps the introduction of formative CAA could be presented as an activity which would complement this aim.

Appendix E provides a model for the introduction of CAA. It offers a structured pathway through the pedagogical, operational, technical and organisational issues which may need to be addressed in order to implement CAA. The model provides both an overarching perspective as well as practical activities.

Key individuals

As suggested earlier in this chapter, the introduction of CAA across an institution requires the support and collaboration of key individuals. The way CAA is used will, in part, dictate who these individuals are. They would probably include senior representatives from some or all of the following areas: relevant academic departments, computing services, staff development, learning and teaching committee (or equivalent), quality assurance, examinations office, senior management team. Additionally, if the institution has units or departments devoted to educational research and development and/or the use of learning technologies, representative(s) from these groups should also be included in discussions.

Members from all relevant groups should be involved in the consultation process of evaluating, selecting and introducing a CAA system into the institution or faculty. Some participants may then be involved in an advisory and policy-making capacity, while others may contribute to the support of staff and students, delivery and administration of assessments.

Particular responsibilities that should be addressed include:

- staff support – pedagogic and technical
- evaluation of software and hardware
- responsibility for computer networks
- timetabling of assessments
- budgeting – start-up and maintenance.

The inclusion of both enthusiasts and sceptics in this group may help create a critical context in which to consider the use of CAA. Enthusiasts might be willing to participate in pilot CAA projects – summative and formative. Individuals who are already using technology and those who teach large first year groups, for whom a reduction in marking would result in considerable savings, might be good candidates for such projects. Those with a more sceptical eye may raise important, critical questions and help anticipate potential problems in the planning stages. Additionally, by involving people with different perspectives and interests early in the consulting

process, there is a greater likelihood that they will feel able to take ownership of, and perhaps even responsibility for, the project, which should
increase its chances of success and disciplinary relevance.

Stimulating discussion about CAA

There are a number of ways to stimulate discussion, debate and research
into CAA, thus raising its profile across the institution:

- Invite outside speakers who can talk about successful CAA systems
  elsewhere. (External experts often help to legitimise the undertaking, and sometimes members of an institution are more receptive
  to a new idea if it comes from someone outside of the organisation
  rather than from a colleague.)
- Present papers at internal research seminars or discussion forums.
- Use external links such as collaborations with other universities,
  government initiatives (such as the development of Teaching and
  Learning strategies), funded educational research projects, and
  agencies such as the Learning and Teaching Support Networks in
  the UK.
- Meet with heads of departments to understand their needs and
  possible concerns about the use of CAA.
- Conduct one-to-one interviews and focus groups with interested
  members of the institution. These will serve to raise awareness of the
  potential and provide valuable feedback. Such work might be
  framed in terms of an educational research project like the one
  described in Chapter 11.
- Run a pilot study with appropriate evaluation to demonstrate feasibility and potential benefits of CAA. Findings can be reported across
  the institution.
- Identify problems for students and academics and consider ways in
  which CAA can offer solutions. These might include the ability to
  provide quick, detailed feedback; time savings in marking; and the
  potential to offer more self-assessment opportunities.
- Introduce CAA into educational development programmes. Offer
  workshops on both technical and pedagogical CAA-related issues:
  question design, constructing and using a varied assessment profile,
  working with test software, analysing CAA results, introducing
  multimedia into assessment practices etc.
- Consider both top-down and bottom-up approaches. Stephens *et al.*
  (1998) argue that a hybrid approach which combines institutional

Table 10.3 Quality assurance recommendations

Integrate the scheduling of computer-based tests into the timetabling for end-of-module examinations.

Ensure the proper moderation of CAA examinations, as for traditional examinations.

Consider appointing an additional, external advisor with expertise in the construction and presentation of CAA.

Incorporate feedback mechanisms which guide academic staff in the improvement of tests and systems.

Ensure that staff have been offered and have attended the relevant staff development sessions.

Develop a procedure which defines and checks that question banks have been supplemented with a percentage of new questions each year.

Verify that piloting procedures and question analysis (to ensure reliability and validity) have been undertaken.

Establish an upper limit on the amount of CAA examination per module. (For example, in order to encourage lecturers to offer a balanced assessment profile to students, the use of CAA might be capped at 40 per cent of the total module mark.)

Agree standards (in terms of screen design, instructions within test, function of buttons) to guarantee consistency in presentation of tests thereby minimising student confusion (King, 1997).

Integrate a programme of evaluation covering all aspects of the system.

(McKenna and Bull, 2000)

strategic support (top-down) with the enthusiasm and innovation of individuals and departments (bottom-up) may aid the development and growth of CAA systems.

The adoption of such techniques may depend on an individual institution's culture and organisational structure. What works well in one institution may not be so successful in a different institution.

For more detailed information about the dynamics of institutional change and the impact on individuals, see Knight's chapter on 'Change, experiencing change and making change happen' (2002a), Knight and Trowler (1998) and Smith (1998).

Quality assurance

When extending the use of CAA, a set of specific quality assurance measures guiding security, feedback to lecturers, support and question development can provide reassurance that a structured system is in place. Depending on institutional regulations, the implementation of CAA for purely formative or self-assessment purposes may require no special quality considerations. However, where summative assessment is conducted, there is a direct impact on student marks and the stakes for successful development, delivery and security of CAA examinations are high. It is therefore crucial that appropriate quality assurance procedures are developed early and appropriate staff development is available to support pedagogical and technical fitness for purpose of the system(s).

To date, relatively little has been done in UK HE to develop quality assurance regulations for the use of CAA for summative examinations. The 1999 CAA Centre National Survey found that only one of the 25 participating quality assurance staff reported having separate examination regulations in place for the governance of CAA (McKenna and Bull, 2000). Such regulations, which should cover the pedagogical, operational and procedural aspects of CAA, not only provide safeguards for lecturers and students, but can also inspire confidence in the system. Quality assurance regulations can be integrated with pre- and post-exam preparations, staff development provision and the evaluation of questions and the system itself. Table 10.3 provides a list of quality assurance recommendations.

Chapter 11

Evaluation

This chapter outlines the importance of evaluating and researching the process of implementing CAA and identifies particular areas where evaluation may be focused.

Introduction

> Evaluation is any activity that throughout the planning and delivery of innovation programmes enables those involved to learn and make judgements about the starting assumptions, implementation processes and outcomes of the innovation concerned.
>
> Stern (1998)

Evaluation of an innovation involves providing enough evidence upon which to make a judgement concerning its effectiveness and appropriateness, and as such, it has much in common with the assessment of learning. Judgements made are likely to include the extent to which an innovation or new technique has met its identified aims and it is, therefore, important to identify those aims at the point of planning the innovation. The match between outcomes and aims provides one measure of the success of an innovation; however, it is important to recognise that unexpected outcomes are often achieved, and in this respect, flexibility should be a feature of any evaluation strategy. Indeed, evaluation may also be a much more open activity which attempts to elicit responses to an approach to learning without confining itself to a consideration of aims and objectives.

Evaluation of CAA

The evaluation of CAA would seem to be a largely neglected activity (Bull et al., 2002; McKenna and Bull, 2000). Of the evaluation that has been undertaken into the efficacy of CAA, much seems to involve the analysis and comparison of examination scores. If existing test questions from paper-based assessments are computerised, then a direct comparison of scores between the two methods might be possible. However, questions are likely to change substantially as a CAA system is introduced and thus direct comparisons are often not possible between paper and computer-based assessments. A related approach has been to attempt to triangulate CAA results with essay and examination scores (Kniveton, 1996; Farthing and McPhee, 1999; Perkin, 1999).

Students' experience of CAA can be analysed across a range of criteria. A hybrid methodology using quantitative and qualitative evaluation can assess student response to CAA as a learning aid, particularly if used as a formative tool (Dalziel and Gazzard, 1999). Questionnaires and interviews can also help to determine whether regular use of CAA affects students' study behaviour (Mulligan, 1999) and to measure student anxiety when performing summative CAA (Pritchett and Zakrzewski, 1996). Additionally, the quality and speed of feedback to students can be compared across paper-based and CAA systems (Bull, 1993). Studies have also considered students' perceptions of CAA, which are generally positive, but do reveal differences in attitude between different groups. Ricketts and Wilks (2002) conducted a study of students' attitudes towards online examinations in biology, business, geography and computing. They found that in all subjects except geography, students were strongly in favour of online examinations and found them acceptable. The geography students were divided approximately in half between those who were in favour of online examinations and those who were not. The study found no significant difference in the overall preparation of students, similar levels of performance improvement between groups and similar IT skills. The authors reflect that wider factors, such as popularity of the module and lecturer, may well account for the difference in attitude towards online examinations.

Mulligan (1999), in an investigation into the impact of regular CAA on study behaviour, reports a noticeable improvement in the work rates of students. McGuire et al. (2002) evaluate the role of partial credit within CAA and paper-based examinations. The mode of delivery is also explored by Fiddes et al. (2002), who found no statistically significant difference in performance between paper and screen tests, but interestingly discovered variation in performance between two sets of paper tests: the original paper-based assessment and the printed-out screen version. In the

US, the Educational Testing Service, responsible for large-scale national testing, has conducted in-depth and large-scale evaluative studies of a range of issues relating to CAA. These studies cover many aspects of testing, including adaptive testing, item response theory, patterns of gender difference, testing of reasoning and cognitive skills, attitudes towards different tests and impact of screen design. (For more information, see http://www.ets.org/research/newpubs.html, accessed January 2003.)

At an institutional or faculty level, evaluation may be concerned with issues of cost, such as efficiency gains in writing, marking and administering assessments, and financial comparisons between CAA and traditional examining methods. (See Dalziel and Gazzard, 1999, for a rudimentary financial analysis of the implementation of WebMCQ at the University of Sydney.) Uptake by students and staff could also form the basis for institutional or faculty evaluations and where sufficient numbers and data were available, the impact of CAA upon retention rate, number of student appeals (Bull,1993) and recruitment could also be explored.

Evaluating learning technology

As the experience of evaluating CAA is limited, it is necessary to take a broader view of evaluation and consider approaches adopted for learning technology generally. There are two main purposes of evaluating learning technology: to measure the educational benefit of introducing learning technology and to assess the cost-effectiveness. This chapter concentrates on evaluating the educational benefit of learning technology.

Oliver and Conole (1998) summarise the difficulties associated with using and evaluating learning technology:

> The effect of IT is not consistent across subject or age groups (Hammond, 1994); high and low ability learners benefit from different types of software (Atkins, 1993); lack of expertise amongst students or teachers can create difficulties (Hammond, 1994); and it can be extremely difficult even to specify or measure 'educational value' (Mason, 1992).

These challenges apply equally to the evaluation of CAA, with the added dimension that assessment can be both culturally and politically sensitive and involves issues of power and control from both an academic and student perspective (McKenna, 2001) (see also Chapter 2). It can be quite difficult to gain a measure or account of such complex dynamics through standard evaluation techniques.

The purpose of evaluation

The purpose of evaluation should generally be determined early in the implementation process. By defining the purpose, appropriate methods and strategies can be developed and planned. It is highly unlikely that every aspect of the implementation of learning technology can be evaluated; this would present a time-consuming and exhausting task. It is therefore useful to focus on particular questions or topics when designing the evaluation, while not excluding the possibility that other areas of interest may emerge during the course of the evaluation.

Most evaluations are driven by the need to provide feedback to those involved with the introduction of CAA. It is useful at the outset to identify the different participants and those with a potential interest in the project and their expectations and priorities when formulating an evaluation strategy.

Types of evaluation

There are many ways of evaluating CAA. Some approaches are particularly focused, aiming to evaluate a very specific aspect of CAA, such as student usage rates of self-assessment tests. Other methods are broader, perhaps concerned with gathering experiences and perceptions. The latter approach might be used, for example, to gather staff and student reflections on the introduction of CAA in a particular course. There are a number of functions which evaluation can fulfil. The following roles are described in the literature (Oliver and Conole, 1998; Cronbach, 1982; Draper *et al.*, 1994; Draper *et al.*, 1997); although the terminology may vary, the principles appear to be commonly represented.

- Formative evaluations seek to identify and evaluate the use and impact of CAA with the purpose of feeding evaluative data back into the design of the system. Formative evaluations commonly identify problems with resources and propose solutions (Cronbach, 1982).
- Summative evaluations provide information at a particular point in the implementation process – when a specified stage has been reached. They are often focused on a specific, well-defined question and seek to measure achievement of learning outcomes.
- Illuminative evaluations, originally introduced by Parlett and Hamilton (1972), attempt to discover factors and issues which are important to certain groups of stakeholders, using an observational approach rather than using standard predefined measures. It is common to try to identify and explain problems in adoption of

educational techniques using illuminative evaluation combined with comparative approaches (Draper *et al.*, 1994).

- Integrative evaluation takes a broad approach to the adoption of learning technology. The aim is to find ways of improving learning, teaching and assessment generally through the introduction of technology. Draper *et al.* (1997) propose that integrative evaluation is 'formative evaluation of the overall teaching situation' which leads towards change in the form of the beneficial integration of learning technology. Illuminative and integrative evaluations are often conducted hand-in-hand, as the former often provides the basis for the latter.

Methods

The list below outlines a variety of evaluation techniques and is taken from the Learning Technology Dissemination Initiative's *Evaluation Cookbook* (Heriot Watt University).

- *Checklists* A quick way of getting a lot of information about an implementation: data gathering is efficient, and collection and analysis can be automated. While a large amount of data can be gathered in this way, it is generally less rich than the information that can be produced through qualitative methods.
- *Concept maps* A concept map or a mind map is a visual representation of the links or associations between different concepts or pieces of information.
- *Confidence logs* These are self-assessment measures which are used to gauge a student's confidence level in a particular topic or part of a course.
- *Ethnography* The essence of an ethnographic approach is 'in situ' observation. The events being observed should be as little disturbed and as authentic as possible.
- *Focus groups* Focus groups are moderated meetings of 'involved' people discussing their experience of an educational intervention. They are a useful tool for formative/developmental or summative/ retrospective evaluation and can serve as a single, self-contained method or link to other evaluation activities.
- *Interviews* Interviews have been described as 'conversations where the outcome is a co-production of the interviewer and the interviewee' (Kvale, 1996). They can be highly structured or very unstructured, depending on the type of information sought.
- *Pre- and post-testing* Pre- and post-testing involves collecting data

(usually by questionnaire) before and after an intervention to provide a measure of its impact.

- *Questionnaires*   A collection of open or closed questions which can be paper-based or online.
- *Resource questionnaires*   Resource questionnaires seek to identify which resources students are using.
- *Split screen video*   Involves video recording the student and the software in use.
- *Supplemental observation*   This involves watching how your students make use of a piece of software.
- *System log data*   System log data is a step-by-step recording of user interaction with a software program. The level of detail recorded is determined by a purpose-built program and can include mouse clicks, menu calls and all operations on objects. Modelled on a 'record' facility, log data is a useful way of tracking user preferences and navigational choices.
- *Trials*   Planning trials allows you to pace the introduction of new techniques with your students. You can decide at what stages you need to test your developments, and who can give you the right sort of feedback so that improvements can be made. Once trials are in your plan, they also become a deadline to work to and can make all the difference between something that is really used and something that looks nice, but never gets put in front of any student.

Cook (2002) provides a good overview of the range of methodologies which can be used to evaluate CAA, while the Evaluating Learning Technology toolkit (Oliver and Conole, 1998) provides a practical, guided methodology.

Quantitative and qualitative approaches

Quantitative approaches to evaluation depend upon the collection of data, such as student grades, usage rates, statistical analysis (such as discrimination and facility) and error reports, as well as data derived from closed question surveys. Qualitative approaches involve using techniques which result in attitudinal and experiential findings. Examples include confidence logs, diaries, semi-structured or unstructured interviews, focus groups and open-ended questions as part of a survey. Qualitative techniques are more fluid and less predictable and controllable than quantitative methods, and they tend to yield fuller and more complex results.

There are benefits and limitations to both quantitative and qualitative techniques which are discussed in detail in Clark (1999), Patton (1990), Seale (1999) and Pawson and Tilley (1997). Evaluation often involves using a combination of methods that complement each other, in order to amplify different aspects of the learning technology.

Choosing a method

Each method represents a different approach to evaluation and no one method is sufficient to evaluate all aspects of an innovation. The most appropriate tool will depend on the particular purpose of the evaluation.

The importance of defining what you wish to evaluate cannot be underestimated. Small variations in wording or process can have considerable impact. Asking, 'What factors influence how students perform at CAA?' suggests an exploratory study which seeks to identify influences on performance. However, asking, 'Which of the following factors influences how students perform at CAA?' suggests a comparative study, possibly involving a controlled experiment.

The extent to which the evaluation is exploratory is likely to determine the methods used. Asking 'what' questions may indicate that few preconceptions of the answers are held, and that the investigation is largely exploratory. In the example above, the factors that will influence learning need to be discovered in the course of the study. By asking 'which' questions, the factors which influence learning have already been identified and the evaluation is conducted to measure their influence on students. In this situation the evaluation is less exploratory. Qualitative methods, which involve more open-ended techniques such as interviews, observations, concept maps and focus groups, are suited to explorative studies. Checklists, experiments and quantitative data collection techniques require a framework for questions to be fixed in advance.

Other factors which influence the selection of methods include:

- *Authenticity*   In some situations it may be appropriate (and more ethical) to test your ideas in a laboratory-like setting, especially if student grades may be affected by an evaluation study. Controlled studies are unsuitable for certain evaluation questions, which depend on a real-life situation.
- *Scale*   The number of people involved in an evaluation may determine, in part, the methods which can be used. For example, it would be impractical to conduct focus groups or interviews with hundreds of students; a questionnaire would be a more realistic solution. In general, approaches which are essentially qualitative in nature are best suited to smaller groups.

- *Topics for evaluation:*
  - comparison of scores between CAA and paper-based tests
  - correlation between CAA tests and other assessment methods within a module or course unit
  - student attitudes towards CAA (ease of use, anxiety, relevance of content, accessibility, perceived equity of system)
  - quality and speed of feedback to students
  - quality of questions
  - effects of CAA on student study behaviour
  - staff attitudes towards CAA (educational efficacy, ease of use, anxiety, use in different educational levels).

Research and evaluation

Many of the evaluation techniques described in this chapter are very similar to (if not the same as) educational research methods, and it might be useful and even preferable in some contexts to frame evaluation studies as small-scale research projects. In some universities, the introduction of new approaches to learning and teaching (such as CAA) is seen in terms of a collaboration between educationalists and subject specialists, and the work is shaped, in part, with a series of research questions in mind which are investigated during the course of the project, often with a view to producing research papers and/or seminars. This work often relies on qualitative investigation and moves beyond a simple tracking of aims against outcomes, to engage with questions of real concern in higher education. Conceived of in this way, it means that negative as well as positive findings are equally valid. Furthermore, in some institutions and disciplines, the research element gives the investigation a certain credibility, and through publication, the work gains a wider audience.

With any innovation, it is advisable to evaluate and research the impact that it has on educational practice and student learning. The high-stakes nature of some assessment means that it is particularly important to consider what impact the introduction of C&IT will have both for students and in terms of the existing assessment methods and strategies and working practices. This chapter has outlined a range of different areas which you may wish to evaluate, depending on the type and purpose of CAA. It is, however, important to be practical about what is achievable in terms of time and resources committed to evaluation. Planning the evaluation realistically from the outset will help to increase the likelihood that it will yield interesting and valuable results.

Conclusion

Originally perceived as a method for delivering objective test questions automatically, CAA is now emerging as a more holistic approach to assessment which, particularly in emergent forms, can offer additional and alternative methods for both formative and summative assessment, and can also introduce variety into the curriculum in terms of assessment type, integration of new media, location of assessment and timing (again, especially with formative CAA).

Nonetheless, CAA imposes certain constraints, as do most learning technologies and indeed most assessment methods, and we would not advocate CAA methods as the sole means by which students are examined. We would also suggest that it has more potential applications in some disciplines (such as computer- and science-based subjects) than other, more discursive, areas of study.

However, in nearly all areas, CAA may improve the authenticity of assessment, since work with computers will almost certainly play a part in what students do during and after leaving university. Looked at in this way, it is the traditional examination (that is, writing with pen and paper for a timed period) which is increasingly unlike the learning students do in the rest of their course. Given that students tend to use word processing packages to write essays and reports, then even the process of composition in the formal exam (one which does not allow the manipulation of text, for example) becomes increasingly a foreign experience. Moreover, the combination of CAA with a more conventional method (such as a viva or presentation) can also aid authenticity in the assessment process.

The introduction of CAA into a department or institution often involves a re-conceptualisation of assessment design. For example, additional approaches to writing and constructing questions and examinations might be adopted. It is also possible that with CAA, student participation in the process (particularly in the shape of self-assessment), and formative activities, which offer increased opportunities for feedback, might feature more prominently in the curriculum. A particular strength of CAA is the ability to offer quick, detailed, albeit standardised, feedback to students at the point of learning. Additionally, as Knight (2002a, 2002b) suggests, a programme-level approach to assessment which values formative as well as summative assignments and considers how different methods might combine to assess a broad range of subject understanding and abilities, is especially valuable for the integration of CAA.

Technologically, CAA is swiftly moving beyond a simple transfer of tests from page to screen, as Bennett (1998) predicted. Mechanisms are emerging to provide ever more sophisticated and authentic assessments which are unique to the medium of delivery. Additionally, at national and international levels, work on interoperability standards should enable greater collaboration and re-use of assessments, offering efficiency gains and yet further development opportunities. However, the rapid growth cycle of technology offers challenges as well as opportunities. The desire to keep pace with technological change should be countered by reflection upon what is educationally sound, practical, affordable and achievable by the staff, students and institution involved. Change (whether technological or otherwise) does not necessarily represent an improved experience for either students or staff. Additionally, even without upgrading software or systems, CAA requires continual investment in technological infrastructures, support – both pedagogical and technical – and, crucially, staff time.

Often the process of introducing CAA prompts a reconsideration of existing assessment methods and strategies, raising questions about purpose, scope, process, delivery, and roles and responsibilities of both staff and students. Heightened awareness of such issues can provide the opportunity to debate the role of assessment in higher education and to explore the appropriateness of both existing and emerging methods. Furthermore, questions should continue to be asked following the adoption of a new method, and the importance of assessment to student learning is such that it necessitates a consideration of what impact CAA will have for students (for example, in terms of learning, control, autonomy, identity), academics, assessment strategies, working practices, educational resources etc. Additionally, we feel that the overall body of educational research into CAA should be expanded and strengthened.

Finally, writing about CAA is a bit like walking through melting snow: the surrounding landscape is constantly changing and, all around, new areas of growth are coming into view. Thus, it is almost inevitable that many of the examples and specific techniques described in this book will be quickly superseded. No doubt, the future will bring assessment techniques which are currently unimaginable. Nonetheless, it seems important to at least try to capture a sense of what CAA has become thus far, and we hope that many of the basic principles and ideas here will be of value for a while to come.

References

American Physical Society (1996) *Fighting the Gender Gap: standardised tests are a poor indicators of ability in physics*, American Physical Society, News On-line, http://www.aps.org/apsnews/0796/11538.html (accessed January 2003).

Angoff, W.H. and Schrader, W.B. (1981) A study of alternative methods for equating right scores to formula scores. Research Report, New Jersey: Educational Testing Service.

Antonelli, M.A. (1997) Accuracy of second-year medical students self-assessment of clinical skills, *Academic Medicine* 72: 563–5.

Askew, S. and Lodge, C. (2000) Gifts, ping-pong and loops – linking feedback and learning, in S. Askew (ed) *Feedback for Learning*, London: Routledge.

Atkins, M. (1993) Evaluating interactive technologies for learning, *Journal of Curriculum Studies* 25(4): 333–42.

Baggott, G. and Rayne, R. (2001) Learning support for mature, part-time, evening students: providing feedback via frequent, computer-based assessments, in M. Danson (ed.) Proceedings of the 5th International Computer-assisted Assessment Conference, 2–3 July 2001, Loughborough: Loughborough University, pp. 9–20, http://www.lboro.ac.uk/service/ltd/flicaa/conferences.html (accessed January 2003).

Baldwin, B.A. and Howard, T.P. (1983) Intertopical sequencing of examination questions: an empirical evaluation, *Journal of Accounting Education* 1(2): 89–96.

Barnett, R. (1995) *Improving Higher Education: total quality care*, Buckingham: Society for Research in Higher Education and Open University Press.

Beevers, C.E., Cherry, B.G., Foster, M.G. and McGuire, G.R. (1991) *Software Tools for Computer Aided Learning in Mathematics*, Aldershot, UK: Ashgate Publishing Ltd.

Beevers, C.E., Foster, M.G., McGuire, G.R. and Renshaw, J.H. (1992) Some Problems of Mathematical CAL, *Journal of Computing Education* 18: 119–25.

Benford, S., Burke, E. and Foxley, E. (1992) Automatic assessment of computer programs in the Ceilidh system, IEEE-SC International Software Metrics Symposium.

Bennett, R.E. (1998) *Reinventing Assessment: speculations on the future of large-scale educational testing*, Research Report. New Jersey: Educational Testing Service. Available from http://www.ets.org/research/newpubs.html (accessed January 2003).

Biometric Consortium (2002) http://www.biometrics.org/ (accessed January 2003).

Bloom, B.S. (ed.), Englehart, M.D., Furst, E.J., Hill, W.H. and Krathwohl, D.R. (1956) *Taxonomy of Educational Objectives: handbook 1: cognitive domain*, New York: Longmans.

Borga, J. (2002) Finger scanning technology monitors school employees, *Education Week on the Web*, October 23, 2002, http://www.edweek.org/ew/ ewstory.cfm?slug=08biometric.h22 (accessed January 2003).

Boud, D. (1995) *Enhancing Learning Through Self-Assessment*, London: Kogan Page.

Boyle, S. (1984) The effect of variations in answer-sheet format on aptitude test performance, *Journal of Occupational Psychology* 57: 323–6.

Brew, A. (1999) Towards autonomous assessment: using self-assessment and peer-assessment, in S. Brown and A. Glasner (1999) *Assessment Matters in Higher Education*, Buckingham: Society for Research in Higher Education.

Brewster, S., Masters M.M. and Glendye, A. (2000) Haptic virtual reality for training veterinary students, paper presented at ED-MEDIA99, Seattle, USA. Available from http://www.dcs.gla.ac.uk/~michelle (accessed January 2003).

Britain, S. and Liber, O. (2000) *A Framework for Pedagogical Evaluation of Virtual Learning Environments*, JISC Technology Applications Programme. Bristol: Joint Information Systems Committee report, http://www.jtap.ac.uk/ reports/htm/jtap-041.html (accessed January 2003).

British Educational Communications and Technology Agency (2001) Computer games in education (CGE) project. http://forum.ngfl.gov.uk/Images/vtc/Games_ and_education/GamesReportfinal.rtf (accessed January 2003).

British Standards Institute (2002) Code of practice for the use of information technology in the delivery of assessments, http://www.bsi-global.com (accessed January 2003).

Brosnan, M. (1999) Computer anxiety in students: should computer-based assessment be used at all? in S. Brown, J. Bull and P. Race (eds) (1999) *Computer-assisted Assessment in Higher Education*, London: Kogan Page.

Brown, G. with Bull, J. and Pendlebury, M. (1997) *Assessing Student Learning in Higher Education*, London: Routledge.

Brown, S. (1999) Assessing practice, in S. Brown and A. Glasner (eds) (1999) *Assessment Matters in Higher Education: Choosing and Using Diverse Approaches*, Buckingham: Society for Research in Higher Education and Open University Press, pp. 95–105.

Bull, J. (1993) *Using Technology to Assess Student Learning*, Sheffield: The Universities' Staff Development Unit and the Universities of Kent and Leeds, TLTP Project ALTER.

Bull, J. and McKenna, C. (2000) CAA centre update, in H. Cooper and S. Clowes (eds) Proceedings of the 4th International Computer-assisted Assessment Conference,

21–22 June 2000, Loughborough: Loughborough University, pp. 11–19 http://www.lboro.ac.uk/service/ltd/flicaa/conferences.html (accessed January 2003).

Bull, J. and Dalziel, J. (2003) Assessing question banks, in A. Littlejohn, *Reusing Resources for Networked Learning*, London: Kogan Page.

Bull, J., Conole, G., Danson, M., Davis, H., Sclater, N. and White, S. (2002) Rethinking assessment through learning technologies, in Proceedings of 18th Annual Conference of the Australasian Society for Computers in Learning in Tertiary Education, 8–11 November 2002, UNITEC, Auckland, New Zealand.

Burbules, N. (1998) Rhetorics of the web: hyperreading and critical literacy, in I. Snyder (1998) *Page to Screen: Taking Literacy into the Electronic Era*, London: Routledge, pp. 102–22.

Burstein, J., Kaplan, R., Wolff, S. and Chi Lu (1996) Using lexical semantic techniques to classify free-response, in Proceedings of SIGLEX 1996 Workshop, Annual Meeting of the Association of Computational Linguistics, University of California, Santa Cruz.

Burstein, J., Kukich, K., Wolff, S., Lu, C. and Chodorow, M. (1998) Enriching automated scoring using discourse marking, in Proceedings of the Workshop on Discourse Relations and Discourse Marking, Annual Meeting of the Association of Computational Linguistics, August 1998, Montreal, Canada.

Burstein, J. and Chodorow, M. (1999) Automated essay scoring for non-native english speakers, Joint Symposium of the Association of Computational Linguistics and the International Association of Language Learning Technologies, Workshop on Computer-Mediated Language Assessment and Evaluation of Natural Language Processing, June 1999, College Park, Maryland.

Burstein, J., Leacock, C. and Swartz, R. (2001) Automated evaluation of essays and short answers, in M. Danson (ed.) Proceedings of the 5th International Computer-assisted Assessment Conference, 2–3 July 2001, Loughborough: Loughborough University, pp. 41–53 http://www.lboro.ac.uk/service/ltd/flicaa/conferences.html (accessed January 2003).

Burstein, J. and Macru, D. (1999) *The Benefits of Modularity in an Automated Essay Scoring System*, Educational Testing Services, available from http://www.ets.org/research/dload/colinga4.pdf (accessed January 2003).

Burton, R. (2001) Quantifying the effects of chance in multiple choice and true/false tests: question selection and guessing of answers, in *Assessment and Evaluation in Higher Education* 26(1): 41–50.

Choppin, B (1979) Testing the questions – the Rasch model and item banking, *MESA Research Memoranda 49*, MESA Psychometric Laboratory, University of Chicago, http://www.rasch.org/memos.htm (accessed January 2003).

Chung, G.K.W.K. and O'Neill, H.F., Jr. (1997) Methodological approaches to on-line scoring of essays. (Delivered to OERI, Award No. R305B60002.) Los Angeles: University of California, National Center for Research on Evaluation, Standards, and Student Testing (CRESST).

Clarke, A. (1999) *Evaluation Research: An introduction to principles, methods and practice*, London: Sage.

Cleave-Hogg, D., Morgan, P. and Guest, C. (2000) Evaluation of medical students performance in anaesthesia using a CAE Med-link simulator system, in H. Cooper and S. Clowes (eds) Proceedings of the 4th International Computer-assisted Assessment Conference, 21–22 June 2001, Loughborough: Loughborough University, pp. 119–28 http://www.lboro.ac.uk/service/ltd/flicaa/conferences.html (accessed January 2003).

Cook, J. (2002) Evaluating learning technology resources guide, Learning and Teaching Support Network, Generic Centre and the Association for Learning Technology, http://www.ltsn.ac.uk/genericcentre/index.asp?id=17149 (accessed January 2003).

Creme, P. (1995) Assessing 'seminar work': students as teachers, in P. Knight (ed) *Assessment for Learning in Higher Education*, London: Kogan Page.

Creme, P. (2000) The personal in university writing: uses of reflective learning journals in M. Lea and B. Stierer (eds) *Student Writing in Higher Education: New Contexts*, Buckingham: Society for Research in Higher Education and Open University Press.

Cronbach, L. (1982) Issues in planning evaluations, in L. Cronbach (ed.), *Designing Evaluations of Educational and Social Programs*, San Francisco: Jossey-Bass.

Cronbach, L.J. (1949) *Essentials of Psychological Testing*, New York: Harper and Row.

Dacre, J. and Haq, I. (2002) Evaluation of a clinical skills website and its effect on student performance. Presentation at Teaching and Learning at University College London http://www.ucl.ac.uk/Library/TL2002 (accessed January 2003).

Daly, C. and Waldron, J. (2002) Introductory programming, problem solving and computer assisted assessment, in M. Danson (ed.) Proceedings of the 6th International Computer-assisted Assessment Conference, 9–10 July 2002, Loughborough: Loughborough University, pp. 95–105 http://www.lboro.ac.uk/service/ltd/flicaa/conferences.html (accessed January 2003).

Dalziel, J. (2001) Enhancing web-based learning with computer assisted assessment: pedagogical and technical considerations, in M. Danson (ed.) Proceedings of the 5th International Computer-assisted Assessment Conference 2–3 July 2001, Loughborough: Loughborough University, pp. 99–107 http://www.lboro.ac.uk/service/ltd/flicaa/conferences.html (accessed January 2003).

Dalziel, J. and Gazzard, S. (1999) Next generation computer assisted assessment software: the design and implementation of WebMCQ in M. Danson and R. Sherratt (eds) Proceedings of the 3rd International Computer-assisted Assessment Conference, 16–17 June 1999, Loughborough: Loughborough University, pp. 61–71 http://www.lboro.ac.uk/service/ltd/flicaa/conferences.html (accessed January 2003).

Davies, P. (2002) There's no confidence in multiple-choice testing … , in M. Danson (ed.) Proceedings of the 6th International Computer-assisted Assessment Conference, 9–10 July 2002, Loughborough: Loughborough University, pp. 119–31 http://www.lboro.ac.uk/service/ltd/flicaa/conferences.html (accessed January 2003).

Dearing, R. (1997) *Higher Education in the Learning Society–Summary Report*, The National Committee of Inquiry into Higher Education, London: HMSO.

Denton, P. (2001) Generating and e-mailing feedback to students using MS Office, in Danson M. (ed.) Proceedings of the 5th International Computer-assisted Assessment Conference 2–3 July 2001, Loughborough: Loughborough University, pp. 157–74 http://www.lboro.ac.uk/service/ltd/flicaa/conferences.html (accessed January 2003).

DTI (2001) *The UK Games Industry and Higher Education*, DTI report, April 2001, http://www.dti.gov.uk/cii/services/contentindustry/games_skills.pdf (accessed January 2003).

Draper, S., Brown, M., Edgerton, E., Henderson, F., McAteer, E., Smith, E., Watt, H. (1994) *Observing and Measuring the Performance of Educational Technology*, TILT Report No. 1, Glasgow: University of Glasgow.

Draper, S., Brown, M., Henderson, F., McAteer, E. (1997) Integrative evaluation: an emerging role for classroom studies of CAL, *Computers in Education* 26(1–3): 17–35.

Drasgow, F. and Oslon-Buchanan, J.B. (1999) *Innovations in Computerised Assessment*, Mahwah, New Jersey: Lawrence Erlbaum Associates.

Ehrmann, S.C. (1998) Studying teaching, learning and technology: a toolkit from the Flashlight program, *Active Learning* 9. 36–8.

Entwistle, N.J., McCune, V. and Hounsell, J. (2002) Approaches to studying and perceptions of university teaching-learning environments: concepts, measures and preliminary findings, Occasional Report No. 1, September, 2002, ETL Project, Universities of Edinburgh, Coventry and Durham. Available from URL: http://www.ed.ac.uk/etl (accessed January 2003).

Evans, A.W., McKenna, C. and Oliver, M. (2002) Self-assessment in medical practice, *Journal of the Royal Society of Medicine* 95: 511–13.

Falchikov, N. (1995) Improving feedback to and from students in P. Knight (ed.) *Assessment for Learning in Higher Education*, London: Kogan Page.

Farthing, D. and McPhee, D. (1999) Multiple choice for honours-level students? A statistical evaluation, in M. Danson and R. Sherratt (eds) Proceedings of the 3rd International Computer-assisted Assessment Conference, 16–17 June 1999, Loughborough: Loughborough University, pp. 105–116 http://www.lboro.ac.uk/service/ltd/flicaa/conferences.html (accessed January 2003).

Fiddes, D.J., Korabinski, A.A., McGuire, G.R., Youngson, M.A. and McMillan, D. (2002) Are mathematics exam results affected by the mode of delivery, *ALT-J* 10: 61–9.

Foltz, P.W. (1996) Latent semantic analysis for text-based research, in *Behavior Research Methods, Instruments and Computers* 28(2): 197–202.

Foxely, E., Higgins, C., Tsintsifas, A. and Symoniedes, P. (1999) The Ceildh Coursemaster System: an introduction, *4th Java in Computing Conference*, LTSN Centre for Information and Computer Sciences http://www.ics.ltsn.ac.uk/pub/Jicc4/foxley.pdf (accessed January 2003).

Foxley, E., Higgins, C., Hegazy, T., Symeonidis, P. and Tsintsifas, A. (2001) The CourseMaster CBA System: improvements over Ceilidh, in M. Danson (ed.) Proceedings of the 5th International Computer-assisted Assessment Conference

2–3 July 2001, Loughborough: Loughborough University, pp. 189–201 http://www.lboro.ac.uk/service/ltd/flicaa/conferences.html (accessed January 2003).

Gardner-Medwin, A.R. (1995) Confidence assessment in the teaching of basic science, in *ALT-J* 3(1).

Gibbs, G. (1999) Using assessment strategically to change the way students learn, in S. Brown and A. Glasner (eds) (1999) *Assessment Matters in Higher Education: choosing and using diverse approaches,* Buckingham: Society for Research in Higher Education and Open University Press.

Glasner, A. (1999) Innovations in student assessment: a system-wide perspective, in S. Brown and A. Glasner (eds) (1999) *Assessment Matters in Higher Education: choosing and using diverse approaches*, Buckingham: Society for Research in Higher Education and Open University Press.

Green, B.F. (1983) Adaptive testing by computer, in R.B. Ekstrom (ed.) *Measurement, Technology, and Individuality in Education: new directions for testing and measurement*, No 17, San Francisco, California: Jossey-Bass.

Gronlund, N.E. (1988) *How to Construct Achievement Tests*, Englewood Cliffs, New Jersey: Prentice Hall.

Grove-Stephenson, I., Sclater, N. and Heath, A. (2002) Building a compliance audit for BS7988 'Code of practice for the use of information technology for the delivery of assessments', in M. Danson (ed.) Proceedings of the 6th International Computer-assisted Assessment Conference, 9–10 July 2002, Loughborough: Loughborough University, pp. 133–36 http://www.lboro.ac.uk/service/ltd/flicaa/conferences.html (accessed January 2003).

Gruber, R.A., (1987) Sequencing exam questions relative to topic presentation, *Journal of Accounting Education*, pp. 77–86.

Haladyna, T.M. (1997) *Writing Test Items to Evaluate Higher Order Thinking*, Boston: Allyn and Bacon.

Halstead, P. (1994) Computer aided learning and assessment for programming skills, *Monitor* 4: 76–8 CTI Centre for Computing.

Hambleton, R.K, Swaminathan, H. and Rogers, H.J. (1991) *Fundamentals of Item Response Theory*, California: Sage Publications.

Hammond, M. (1994) Measuring the impact of IT on learning, *Journal of Computer Assisted Learning* 10: 251–60.

Heard, S., Nicol, J. and Heath, S. (1997a) *Protocol for the Implementation of Summative Computer-assisted Assessment Examinations*, Aberdeen: Mertal Publications, University of Aberdeen.

Heard, S., Nicol, J. and Heath, S. (1997b) *Setting Effective Objective Tests*, Aberdeen: Mertal Publications, University of Aberdeen.

Henkel, M. (2000) *Academic Identities and Policy Change in Higher Education*, London: Jessica Kingsley.

Higgins, R., Hartley, P. and Skelton, A. (2001) Getting the message across: the problem of communicating assessment feedback. Points for debate, in *Teaching in Higher Education* 6(2): 269–74.

Holley, D. and Oliver, M. (2000) Pedagogy and new power relationships, in *The International Journal of Management Education* 1(1): 11–21.

Irving, A., Read, M., Hunt, A. and Knight, S. (2000) Uses of information technology in exam revision, in H. Cooper and S. Clowes (eds) Proceedings of the 4th International Computer-assisted Assessment Conference, 21–22 June 2001, Loughborough: Loughborough University, pp. 99–107 http://www.lboro.ac.uk/service/ltd/flicaa/conferences.html (accessed January 2003).

Isaacs, G. (1994) About multiple choice questions, *Multiple Choice Testing: Green Guide*, No.16, Cambelltown, New South Wales: HERDSA, pp. 4–22.

Jacobs, D. (2002) Personnal communication with the authors. Royal Veterinary College.

Kafai, Y.B. (2001) *The Educational Potential of Electronic Games: from games-to-teach to games-to-learn, playing by the rules*, Chicago: Cultural Policy Center, University of Chicago.

King, T. (1997) Recommendations for managing the implementation of computer aided assessment, *Active Learning*, 6: 23–6.

King, T. and White, I. (1999) A University wide protocol for the conduct of computer assisted assessment, *Technical Report No. 3*, Integrating People and Technology, Fund for the Development of Teaching and Learning project, Portsmouth: University of Portsmouth.

King, T., Billinge, D., Callear D., Wilson, S., Wilson, A. and Briggs, J. (1998) Developing and evaluation a CAA protocol for university students, in W. Wade and M. Danson (eds), Proceedings of the 2nd Annual Computer-assisted Assessment Conference, 17–18 June 1998, Loughborough: University of Loughborough, pp. 17–23 http://www.lboro.ac.uk/service/ltd/flicaa/conferences.html (accessed January 2003).

Kirriemuir, J. (2002a) *The Relevance of Gaming and Gaming Consoles to the Higher and Further Education Learning Experience*, Joint Information Systems Committee, Technology Watch Report, February/March 2002 http://www.jisc.ac.uk/techwatch/reports/tsw_02–01.rtf (accessed January 2003).

Kirriemuir, J. (2002b) Video gaming, education and digital learning technologies, *D-Lib Magazine,* February, 8, 2, http://www.dlib.org/dlib/february02/kirriemuir/02kirriemuir.html (accessed January 2003).

Kneale, P.E. (1997) The rise of the strategic student: how can we adapt to cope? in S. Armstrong, G. Thompson and S. Brown (eds) *Facing up to Radical Changes in Universities and Colleges*, London: Staff and Educational Development Agency, Kogan Page, pp. 119–39.

Knight, P. (2002a) *Being a Teacher in Higher Education*, Buckingham: Society for Research in Higher Education and Open University Press.

Knight, P. (2002b) Summative assessment in higher education: practices in disarray, *Studies in Higher Education* 27(2): 275–86.

Knight, P. and Trowler, P. (2001) *Departmental Leadership in Higher Education*,

Buckingham: Society for Research in Higher Education and Open University Press.

Kniveton, B.H. (1996) A correlation analysis of multiple-choice and essay assessment measures, *Research in Education* 56: 73–84.

Kress, G. (1998) Visual and verbal modes of representation in electronically mediated communication: the potentials of new forms of text, in I. Snyder (1998) *Page to Screen: Taking Literacy into the Electronic Era*, London: Routledge, pp. 53–79.

Kuminek, P.A. and Pilkington, R.M. (2001) Helping the tutor facilitate debate to improve literacy using computer mediated communication, IEEE International Conference on Advanced Learning Technologies: Issues, Achievements and Challenges, Madison, Wisconsin, 6–8 August, IEEE Computer Society, ISBN 0–7695–1013–2.

Kvale, S. (1996) Interviews as knowledge construction, Qualitative Research: Space for Critique and Creativity Symposium, XXVI, *International Congress of Psychology*, Montreal, pp. 1–18.

Land, R. and Bayne, S. (2002) Screen or monitor? Issues of surveillance and disciplinary power in online learning environments, in C. Rust (ed.) Proceedings of Improving Student Learning Conference, Oxford: Oxford Centre for Staff and Learning Development, Oxford Brookes University.

Laurillard, D., Stratfold, M., Luckin, R., Plowman, L. and Taylor, J. (2000) Affordances for learning in a non-linear narrative medium, in *Journal of Interactive Media in Education*, 2, http://www-jime.open.ac.uk/00/2/ (accessed January 2003).

Laurillard, D. (1993) *Rethinking University Teaching: a framework for the effective use of educational technology*, London: Routledge.

Lea, M. (2000) Computer conferencing: new possibilities for writing and learning in Higher Education, in M. Lea and B. Stierer (2000) *Student Writing in Higher Education*, Buckingham: SRHE and Open University Press, pp. 69–85.

Lea, M. (2001) Computer conferencing and assessment, in *Studies in Higher Education* 26(2): 163–79.

Lillis, T. (2001) *Student Writing: Access, regulation, desire*, London: Routledge.

Lillis, T. and Turner, J. (2001) Student writing in higher education: contemporary confusion, traditional concerns, in *Teaching in Higher Education* 6(1): 57–68.

Lord, F. (1970) Some test theory for tailored testing, in Holtzman, W. H. (ed.) Computer-assisted instruction, testing, and guidance, pp. 139–83. New York: Harper Row.

MacDonald, C. (2002) Virtual Private Networks: an overview, in *Intranet Journal*, http://www.intranetjournal.com/foundation/vpn–1.shtml (accessed January 2003).

Mackenzie, D. (1999) Recent development in the Tripartite Interactive Assessment Delivery System (TRIADS) in M. Danson and R. Sherratt (eds) Proceedings of the 3rd International Computer-assisted Assessment Conference, 16–17 June 1999, Loughborough: Loughborough University, pp. 235–50 http://www.lboro.ac.uk/service/ltd/flicaa/conferences.html (accessed January 2003).

Mackenzie, D. and O'Hare, D. (2002) Empirical prediction of the measurement scale and base level 'guess factor' for advanced computer-based assessments, in M. Danson (ed.) Proceedings of the 6th International Computer-assisted Assessment Conference, 9–10 July 2002, Loughborough: University of Loughborough, pp. 187- 201.

Malone, T. (1981) Toward a theory of intrinsically motivating instruction, in *Cognitive Science* 4: 333–69.

Mason, R. (1992) Methodologies for evaluating applications of computer conferencing, *PLUM Report No. 31*, Open University, Milton Keynes.

Massey, A.J. (1995) *Evaluation and Analysis of Examination Data: Some guidelines for reporting and interpretation*, Cambridge: University of Cambridge Local Examination Syndicate, Internal Report.

Matthews, J. (1981) *The Use of Objective Tests*, Lancaster: University of Lancaster Press (revised edn.)

Maughan, S., Peet, D. and Willmott, A. (2001) On-line formative assessment item banking and learning support, in M. Danson (ed.) Proceedings of the 5th International Computer-assisted Assessment Conference 2–3 July 2001, Loughborough: Loughborough University, pp. 335–46 http://www.lboro.ac.uk/service/ltd/flicaa/conferences.html (accessed January 2003).

McAlpine, M. (2001) Using computer-assisted assessment to facilitate resource selection, in M. Danson (ed.) Proceedings of the 5th International Computer-assisted Assessment Conference 2–3 July 2001, Loughborough: Loughborough University, pp. 285–91 http://www.lboro.ac.uk/service/ltd/flicaa/conferences.html (accessed January 2003).

McAlpine, M. (2002a) A summary of methods of item analysis, *Bluepaper Number 2*, Computer-assisted Assessment Centre, http://www.caacentre.ac.uk ISBN 1–904020–02-x (accessed January 2003).

McAlpine, M. (2002b) Design requirements of a databank, *Bluepaper Number 3*, Computer-assisted Assessment Centre, http://www.caacentre.ac.uk ISBN 1–904020–04–6 (accessed January 2003).

McBeath, R.J. (ed.) (1992) *Instructing and Evaluating Higher Education: a guidebook for planning learning outcomes*, Englewood Cliffs, New Jersey: Educational Technology Publications.

McGuire, G.R., Youngson, M.A., Korabinski, A.A. (2002) Partial credit in mathematics exams – a comparison of traditional and CAA exams, in M. Danson (ed.) Proceedings of the 6th International Computer-assisted Assessment Conference, 9–10 July 2002, Loughborough: University of Loughborough, pp. 223–30.

McKenna, C. (2000) Using computers in humanities assessment, in *Computers and Texts* 18/19: 6–7.

McKenna, C. (2001) Who's in control? Considering issues of power and control associated with the use of CAA: a discussion session in M. Danson (ed.) Proceedings of the 5th International Computer-assisted Assessment Conference

2–3 July 2001, Loughborough: Loughborough University, pp. 305–8 http://www.lboro.ac.uk/service/ltd/flicaa/conferences.html (accessed January 2003).

McKenna, C. (2002) What is electronic literacy and where is it best positioned within the academic curriculum?, in C. Rust (ed.) Proceedings of Improving Student Learning Conference, Oxford: Oxford Centre for Staff and Learning Development, Oxford Brookes University.

McKenna, C. and Bull, J. (2000) Quality assurance of computer-assisted assessment: practical and strategic issues, in *Quality Assurance in Higher Education* 8(1): 24–31.

McKenna, C., Loewenberger, P., Bull, J. and Collins, C. (in press) Results of a national survey of computer-assisted assessment, *Bluepaper No. 4*, Computer-assisted Assessment Centre, http://www.caacentre.ac.uk (accessed January 2003).

Meredyth, D., Russell, N., Blackwood, L., Thomas, J. and Wise, P. (1999) Real time, computers, change and schooling, Department of Education Training and Youth Affairs, Commonwealth of Australia. http://www.detya.gov.au/archive/schools/publications/1999/realtime.pdf (accessed January 2003).

Messick, C. (1989) Validity, in R.L. Linn (ed.) (1989) *Educational Measurement* (3rd edn), New York: Macmillan, pp. 13–103.

Morgan, C. and O'Reilly, M. (1994) *Assessing Open and Distance Learners*, London: Kogan Page.

Moss, P.A. (1995) Themes and variations in validity theory, in *Educational Measurement: issues and practice* 14(2): 5–12.

Moss, P.A, (1994) Can there be validity without reliability? *Educational Researcher* 23(2): 5–12.

Mulligan, B. (1999) Pilot study on the impact of frequent computerized assessment on student work rates, in M. Danson and R. Sherratt (eds) Proceedings of the 3rd International Computer-assisted Assessment Conference, 16–17 June 1999, Loughborough: Loughborough University, pp. 137–47 http://www.lboro.ac.uk/service/ltd/flicaa/conferences.html (accessed January 2003).

Newstead, S. and Dennis, I. (1994) Examiners examined: the reliability of exam marking in psychology, *The Psychologist* 7: 216–19.

OCSLD (1994) *Strategies for Diversifying Assessment in Higher Education*, Oxford: Oxford Centre for Staff and Learning Development, Oxford Brookes University.

Oliver, M. and Conole, G. (1998) Evaluating communication and information technologies: a toolkit for practitioners, *Active Learning* 8: 3–8.

Orsmond P., Merry S. and Reiling K. (1997) A study in self-assessment: tutor and students' perceptions of performance criteria, *Assessment and Evaluation in Higher Education* 24(4): 357–69.

Outtz, J.L. (1998) Testing medium, validity and test performance, in M.D. Hakel (1998) *Beyond Multiple Choice: evaluating alternative to traditional testing for selection*, New Jersey: Lawrence Erlbaum Associates.

Page, E.B. and Peterson, N. (1995) The computer moves into essay grading: updating the ancient test, *Phi Delta Kappa*, March: 561–5.

Parlett, M.R. and Hamilton, D. (1972/77/87) Evaluation as illumination: a new approach to the study of innovatory programmes, (1972) workshop at Cambridge, and unpublished report Occasional paper 9, Edinburgh: Centre for Research in the Educational Sciences, University of Edinburgh.

Patton, M.Q. (1990) *Qualitative Evaluation and Research Methods*, London: Sage.

Pawson, R. and Tilley, N. (1997) *Realistic Evaluation*, London: Sage.

Paxton, M. (2000) A linguistic perspective on multiple choice questioning, in *Assessment and Evaluation in Higher Education* 25(2): 109–19.

Pennington, M.C. (1996) Writing the natural way on computer, *Computer Assisted Language Learning* 9: 2–3, 125–42.

Perkin, M. (1999) Validating formative and summative assessment in S. Brown, J. Bull, and P. Race (eds) *Computer-Assisted Assessment in Higher Education*, London: Kogan Page, pp. 57–70.

Pincas, A. (2000) New literacies and future educational culture, in *ALT-J* 8(2): 69–79.

Pritchett, N. and Zakrzewski, S. (1996) Interactive computer assessment of large groups: student responses, *Innovations in Education and Training International* 33(3): 242–7.

Proctor, A. and Donoghue, D. (1994) Computer based assessment: a case study in geography, in *Active Learning* 1 December: 29–34.

Race, P. (1999) Why assess innovatively? in S. Brown and A. Glasner (eds) (1999) *Assessment Matters in Higher Education*, Buckingham: Society for Research in Higher Education and Open University Press.

Ramsden, P. (1992) *Learning to Teach in Higher Education*, Routledge: London.

Rasch, G. (1980). *Probabilistic Models for some Intelligence and Attainment Tests*, Chicago: University of Chicago Press (original work published 1960).

Reynolds, M. and Trehan, K. (2000) Assessment: a critical perspective, *Studies in Higher Education* 25(3): 267–78.

Ricketts, C. and Wilks, S. (2002) What factors affect student opinions of computer-assisted assessment? in M. Danson (ed.) Proceedings of the 6th International Computer-assisted Assessment Conference, 9–10 July 2002, Loughborough: Loughborough University, pp. 307–16 http://www.lboro.ac.uk/service/ltd/flicaa/conferences.html (accessed January 2003).

Robinson, J. (1999) Computer-assisted peer review in S. Brown, J. Bull, and P. Race (eds), *Computer-Assisted Assessment in Higher Education*, London: Kogan Page.

Rowland, S. (2000) *The Enquiring University Teacher*, Buckingham: Society for Research in Higher Education and Open University Press.

Royal College of Physicians (2002) MRPC (UK) Part One and Part Two Written Examinations: introduction of new format, http://www.mrcpuk.org/plain/changes.html (accessed January 2003).

Rudner, L. (1998) An on-line, interactive, computer adaptive testing mini-tutorial, ERIC Clearinghouse on Assessment and Evaluation Digest, http://www.eriche.org/ (accessed January 2003).

Schmidt, N.G., Norman, G.R. and Boshuzen, H.P.A. (1990) A cognitive perspective on medical expertise: theory and implications, *Academic Medicine* 65: 611–21.

Sclater, N., Low, B. and Barr, N. (2002) Interoperability with CAA: does it work in practice? in M. Danson (ed.) Proceedings of the 6th International Computer-assisted Assessment Conference, 9–10 July 2002, Loughborough: Loughborough University, pp. 317–27 http://www.lboro.ac.uk/service/ltd/flicaa/conferences.html (accessed January 2003).

Seale, C. (1999) *The Quality of Qualitative Research*, London: Sage Publications.

Shetzer, H. and Warschauer, M. (2000) An electronic literacy approach to network-based language teaching, in M. Warschauer and R. Kern (eds) (2000) *Network-based Language Teaching: concepts and practice*, New York: Cambridge University Press.

Smith, B. (1998) Adopting a strategic approach to managing change in learning and teaching in M. Kaplan (ed.) *To Improve the Academy*, 18, Stillwater, OK: New Forums Press and the Professional and Organizational Development Network in Higher Education.

Snyder, I. (1998) *Page to Screen: Taking Literacy into the Electronic Era*, London: Routledge.

Stephens, D., Bull, J. and Wade, W. (1998) Computer-assisted assessment: suggested guidelines for an institutional strategy, *Assessment and Evaluation in Higher Education* 23(3): 283–94.

Stephens, D., Sargent, G. and Brew, I. (2001) Comparison of assessed work marking software: implications for the ideal Integrated Marking Tool (IMT) in M. Danson (ed.) Proceedings of the 5th International Computer-assisted Assessment Conference 2–3 July 2001, Loughborough: Loughborough University, pp. 471–86 http://www.lboro.ac.uk/service/ltd/flicaa/conferences.html (accessed January 2003).

Stern E. (1998) *The Evaluation of Policy and the Policies of Evaluation*, Tavistock Institute of Human Relations Annual Review, London: Tavistock Institute.

Stout, D.E. and Wygal, D.E. (1994) Additional empirical evidence on the relationship between exam sequencing and accounting student performance, *Advances in Accounting* 8: 133–52.

Stuart, S. (2002) An electronically enhanced philosophy learning environment, paper presented at Computing and Philosophy Conference. 8–10 August 2002, Carnegie Mellon.

Tait, H. and Entwistle, N. (1996) Identifying students at risk through ineffective study strategies in *Higher Education* 31: 97–116.

Taylor, C., Jamieson, J., Eignor, D. and Kirsch, I. (1998) The relationship between computer familiarity and performance on computer-based TOEFL test tasks, Research Report 61, March, New Jersey: Educational Testing Service, ftp://ftp.ets.org/pub/toefl/275757.pdf (accessed January 2003).

Thissen, D., Wainer, H. and Wang, S.–B. (1994) Are tests comprising both multiple-choice and free-response items necessarily less unidimensional than multiple-choice tests? An analysis of two tests, in *Journal of Educational Measurement*, 31(2): 113–23.

Vermunt, J.D. (1998) The regulation of constructive learning processes in *British Journal of Educational Psychology*, 68: 149–71.

Vermunt, J.D. and Verloop, N. (1999) Congruence and friction between learning and teaching in *Learning and Instruction*, 9: 257–80.

Wainer, H. (2000) *Computerised Adaptive Testing: a primer*, New Jersey: Lawrence Erlbaum Associates.

Ward, W.C., Frederiksen, N. and Carlson, S.B. (1980) Construct validity of free-response and machine-scorable forms of a test, *Journal of Educational Measurement* 7(1):11–29.

Whittington, C.D. and Campbell, L.M. (1999) Task-oriented learning on the web, *Innovations in Education and Training International* 36:1: 26–33.

Wood, J. and Burrow, M. (2002) Formative assessment in engineering using 'TRIADS' software, in M. Danson (ed.) Proceedings of the 6th International Computer-assisted Assessment Conference, 9–10 July 2002, Loughborough: Loughborough University, pp. 369–380 http://www.lboro.ac.uk/service/ltd/flicaa/conferences.html (accessed January 2003).

Wright, B.D. and Bell, S.R. (1984) Item banks: what, why, how, *Memoranda 43*, MESA Psychometric Laboratory, Chicago: University of Chicago http://www.rasch.org/memo43.htm (accessed January 2003).

Zakrzewski, S. and Bull, J. (1998) The mass implementation and evaluation of computer-based assessments, *Assessment and Evaluation in Higher Education* 23:2: 141–52.

Appendix A

Example questions

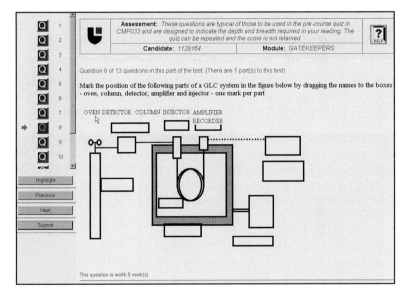

Figure A1 Analytical chemistry: Roger M Smith, Department of Chemistry, Loughborough University

Note
Images for Figures A1–A14 are copyright Loughborough University.

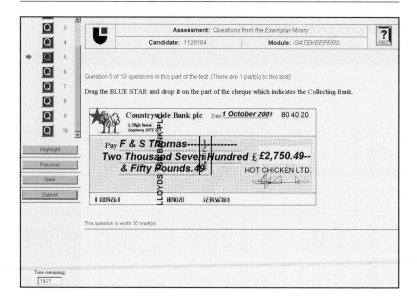

Figure A2 Banking: Keith Pond, Business School, Loughborough University

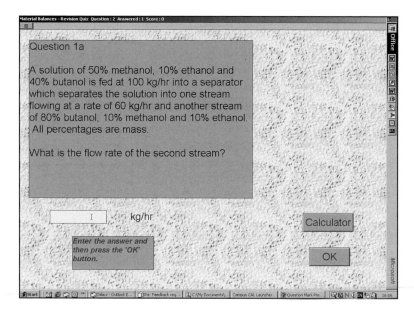

Figure A3 Chemical engineering: David Edwards, Chemical Engineering, Loughborough University

Figure A4 Civil engineering 1: Engineering Teaching and Learning Support Centre, Loughborough University

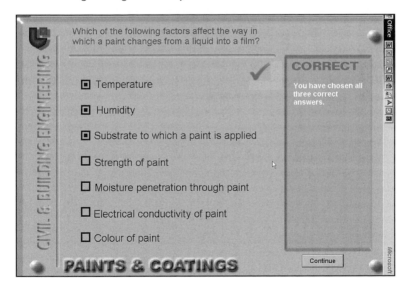

Figure A5 Civil engineering 2: Engineering Teaching and Learning Support Centre, Loughborough University

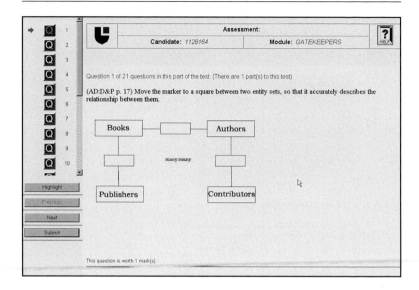

Figure A6 Database design: David Percek and Derek Stephens, Information Science, Loughborough University

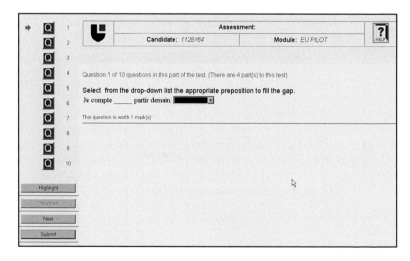

Figure A7 French: Valerie Boyle, European Studies, Loughborough University

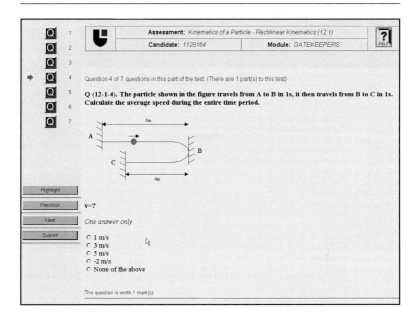

Figure A8 Kinematics: Memis Acar, Mechanical Engineering, and Engineering Teaching and Learning Support Centre, Loughborough University

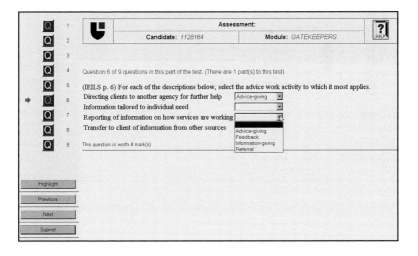

Figure A9 Librarianship: David Percek and Derek Stephens, Information Science, Loughborough University

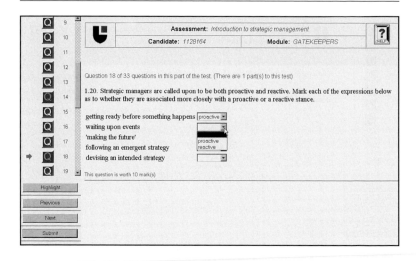

Figure A10   Management 1: Paul Finlay, Business School, Loughborough University

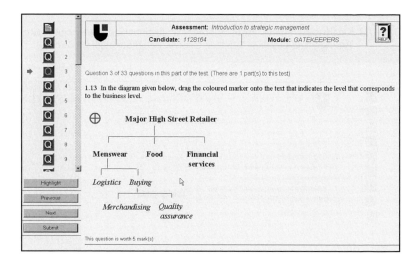

Figure A11   Management 2: Paul Finlay, Business School, Loughborough University

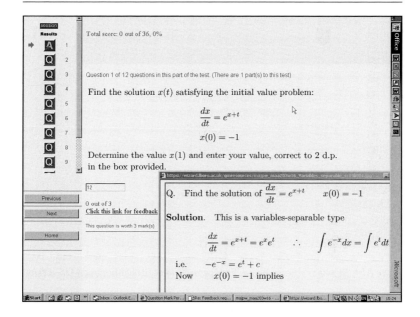

Figure A12 Maths: Joe Ward, Mathematical Sciences, Loughborough University

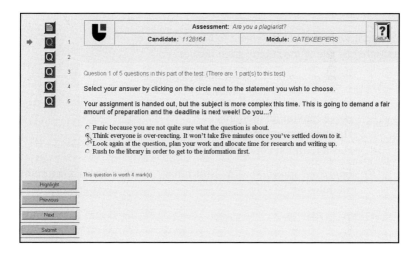

Figure A13 Plagiarism: Ruth Stubbings, Pilkington Library, Loughborough University

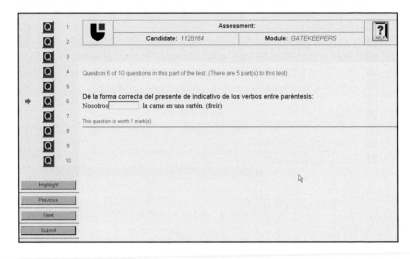

Figure A14 Spanish: Valerie Boyle, European Studies, Loughborough University

In Chapter 4, good practice guidelines were provided on the writing of stems and distracters. The following additional examples exhibit application of the guidelines and were contributed by the Electrical and Electronic Assessment Network (http://www.ecs.soton.ac.uk/E3AN).

Present a single definite statement to be completed or answered by one of the several given choices

    A   *Weak question* – A 4-bit binary counter:

    a   Doesn't have 4 flip-flops
    b   Has a maximum modulus of 8
    c   Has a maximum modulus of 16
    d   Has a terminal count of 15

    B   *Improved question* – A 4-bit binary counter has a maximum modulus of:

    a   4
    b   8
    c   15
    d   16
    e   32

Avoid unnecessary and irrelevant material

A   *Weak question* – The full-adder circuit adds three one-bit binary numbers (C A B) and outputs two one-bit binary numbers, a sum (S) and a carry (C1). The full-adder is usually a component in a cascade of adders, which add 8, 16, 32 etc binary numbers. If you were to feed in the binary number 110 into such a device, the result would be:

a   Sum = 0, carry = 0
b   Sum = 0, carry = 1
c   Sum = 1, carry = 0
d   Sum = 1, carry = 1

B   *Improved question* – The binary number 110 is fed into a full-adder, the result is which of the following:

a   Sum = 0, carry = 0
b   Sum = 0, carry = 1
c   Sum = 1, carry = 0
d   Sum = 1, carry = 1

Use clear, straightforward language in the stem of the item to ensure that the question addresses subject matter rather than acting as a test of reading comprehension

A   *Weak question* – As mortality rates approach the zenith, what is the most likely ramification for the citizenry of an industrial nation?

a   an increase in the labour force participation rate of older people
b   a dispersing effect on population concentration
c   an upward trend in the youth dependency ratio
d   a broader base in the population pyramid
e   an increase in fertility

B   *Improved question* – A major increase in mortality rates in an industrial nation is likely to cause:

a   an increase in the labour force participation rate of older people
b   a dispersing effect on population concentration
c   an upward trend in the youth dependency ratio
d   a broader base in the population pyramid
e   an increase in fertility

Use negatives sparingly. If negatives must be used, capitalise,
underscore, embolden or otherwise highlight

> A   *Weak question* – Which of the following is not the cause of a
> compile-time error in a Java class file?

> a   Missing the semi-colon off the end of a statement
> b   Not including a 'main' method
> c   Using a variable that is not declared
> d   Returning an integer result from a void method

> B   *Improved question* – Which of the following will compile
> successfully?

> a   A statement that has no semi-colon to terminate it.
> b   A class file that is missing a main method
> c   Code that uses a variable that has not been declared
> d   A void method that returns an integer result

Put as much of the question in the stem as possible, rather
than duplicating material

> A   *Weak question* – Calculate the voltage V_x

> a   Using Kirchoff's voltage law V_x is –32V
> b   Using Kirchoff's voltage law V_x is +28V
> c   Using Kirchoff's voltage law V_x is +32V
> d   Using Kirchoff's voltage law V_x is –28V

> B   *Improved question* – For the circuit shown, use Kirchoff's
> voltage law to calculate the voltage source V_x

> a   –32V
> b   +32V
> c   –28V
> d   +28V

For single-response multiple-choice questions, ensure that there
is only one correct response

> A   *Weak question*

Import java.io*;
Class FileHandling {
Public static void main (String [] args) throws Exception {

```
File f = new File ("temp.tmp");
FileOutputSteam s = new FileOutputStream(f);
PrintStream p = new PrintStream(s);
p.println("Hello World");
  }
}
```

If one attempted to compile and run the above Java program:

   a   it would fail to compile
   b   it would execute without error
   c   it would generate a run-time error on execution
   d   it would print 'Hello World' on the standard output (screen)
   e   It would print 'Hello World' to a file called temp.tmp

   B   *Improved question*

```
Import java.io*;
Class FileHandling {
Public static void main (String [] args ) throws Exception {
  File f = new File ("temp.tmp");
  FileOutputSteam s = new FileOutputStream(f);
  PrintStream p = new PrintStream(s);
  p.println("Hello World");
  }
```

If one attempted to compile and run the above Java program, it would:

   a   fail to compile
   b   generate a run-time error on execution
   c   execute, but ask the user to specify the directory in which to create temp.tmp
   d   execute without error and print 'Hello World' on the standard output (screen)
   e   execute without error and print 'Hello World' to a file called temp.tmp

Use only plausible and attractive alternatives as distracters

   A   *Weak question* – A narrative, English-like description of the logic of a programme is called:

   a   Hypertext
   b   A storyboard

c   Pseudocode

d   Fiction

e   Rhetoric

B   *Improved question* – A narrative, English-like description of the logic of a programme is called:

a   Hypertext

b   A storyboard

c   Pseudocode

d   A structure chart

e   An overview diagram

Avoid giving clues to the correct answer

A   *Weak question* – The negatively charged fundamental particle is called an:

a   proton

b   electron

c   neutron

d   quark

B   *Improved question* – The negatively charged fundamental particle is called a/an:

a   proton

b   electron

c   neutron

d   quark

Optical data capture CAA

This appendix provides additional information about the use of optical data-capture technologies for CAA. It draws particularly on the experiences of the development and implementation of a large-scale OMR service at Loughborough University and has been contributed by Myles Danson, CAA Manager, Loughborough University.

Example documentation

Forms

Examples of optical input forms for OMR CAA are included at the end of this appendix. Alternative designs may be desirable and should be supported through OMR software and hardware. The examples are of generic forms; the test paper must fit the optical answer sheet design. It is, of course, possible to make the optical answer design fit the test paper. This would require additional resources of staff time, form design software, and possibly a high-quality laser printer. This scenario is most often seen in standard examinations such as those undertaken by medical schools. Often a form is printed for each candidate, including the candidate authentication detail. This is desirable, as common mark-up errors in this area can be extremely problematic. Paper specification is important if using an automatic feed reader. The correct paper tolerance will permit efficient separation of the scripts and can result in a two script per second feed rate.

Combined OCR/ICR/OMR systems are far more flexible in terms of form design, printing techniques and the tolerance of auto-fed scanning to the condition of the forms. An OMR-only auto-fed system will reject forms which are in poor condition. A combined OCR/ICR/OMR system will tolerate these to a greater extent. Error trapping mechanisms are essential and should not be underestimated. This process becomes essential when reading characters and handwriting and the extent to which this is necessary should be investigated fully. A guarantee of 100 per cent accuracy of data capture is difficult to attain.

Generally, all optical CAA systems will require one *answer sheet* for each student. These should contain a mechanism for student identification (ideally a unique identifier) and a section for question response. In the case of the example forms, the Student Answer Sheet and Examination Answer Sheet use the Student ID Number. It is likely that these are already issued to students upon enrolment and are held in a central database along with other information such as real name and degree programme code. A look-up action allows inclusion of such extra details at the post-processing stage. Alternative approaches require the manual mark-up of student name by each candidate. This requires a great deal of space on the form for alphabetical input and is not guaranteed to be a unique identifier (students taking a test may have the same name). We include two types of answer sheet in the examples, one for summative assessment anonymised for examinations, one for formative assessment (including student name). The answer sheet includes spaces to write the examination/test title, date and seat number (if applicable). There are also spaces for the following information:

- *Candidate number* The student's ID number. This information must be completed. This is the only automated method of identifying candidates. It is a seven-digit number and is written in the boxes along the top of this section. The appropriate numbered area beneath each written digit must be *scored* through, in order that the data can read by the OMR.
- *Question responses* A series of 60 question numbers, with five choice boxes (A, B, C, D, E) against each. This is the final part of the answer sheet which is read by the optical mark reader. A traditional test paper is produced to accompany the answer sheets. This must correspond to the restrictions imposed by the answer sheet design (maximum of 60 questions, distracters labelled A, B, C, D, E).

Generally, all optical CAA systems will require a method of inputting the correct answers in order that student scripts can be marked correct or incorrect. Included with the example forms is the Lecturer Answer Sheet. This is the sheet containing the correct answers, to be completed by the lecturer. It is similar in format to the Student Answer Sheet with the name space overprinted with the word 'Lecturer'. One Lecturer Answer Sheet is required for each set of answers.

Also included is a Batch Header Sheet. This sheet provides additional information used for marking and for inclusion in the reporting. It has spaces for writing in the department name, lecturer name, examination/ test title and test number. There are also spaces for the following information to be entered by the lecturer:

- *Department code*   Two alphabetic characters (CM = Chemistry).
- *Module code*   This uniquely identifies the module.
- *Date of test*   The format for this is dd/month/yy.
- *No. of forms returned*   The number of Student Answer Sheets submitted.
- *Test number*   If the test is one of a series in a module, this will identify the test to which the results refer.
- *The marking schedule*   A set of three fields which will enable the lecturer to specify how the test is marked. Each of the fields can be set at any number from +5 to –5.

In each of the above, the information is written into the boxes at the top of each section, then the appropriate labelled area beneath each is scored out.

Codes of practice

I Use of the OMR CAA system in undergraduate and postgraduate examinations

The Internal Examiner wil undertake training in the use of the OMR system with the CAA Officer prior to utilising the system. Thereafter the Internal Examiner will inform the CAA Officer of his/her intention to use the OMR system, along with module code, number of candidates and week number. This to be undertaken at least eight weeks in advance of the examination session.

- The CAA Officer will supply the required number of Student Answer Sheets to the Examinations Office, and the Lecturer and Batch Header Sheets to the Internal Examiner.
- The Examinations Office will supply the Student Answer Sheets on the day of the examination.
- The Internal Examiner will verbally remind candidates of the OMR procedure at the final lecture of the Module using the information pack supplied by the CAA Officer. No further instruction, verbal or otherwise, shall be given to candidates in the Examination Hall.

- Candidates must provide their own pencils and erasers for the examination.
- The Internal Examiner will cater for the requirements of any students with disabilities or additional needs taking the test after seeking advice from the University Disability and Additional Needs Service.
- The Internal Examiner (or his/her nominated representative) invigilating at the Examination will collect the Student Answer Sheets at the end of the Examination, checking that they are in good condition (not stapled, tagged, folded, torn etc).
- The Internal Examiner is responsible for the collection of the OMR Student Answer Sheets from the Examination Hall or the Examinations Office.
- The Internal Examiner will be responsible for arranging processing of the Student Answer Sheets with Computing Services (see attached Service Level Statement).
- Computing Services will provide a secure system for processing (see attached Service Level Statement).
- The Internal Examiner is responsible for the hand marking of any Student Answer Sheets rejected by the OMR System. A sample of the OMR scripts should be hand marked by another member of academic staff.
- The CAA Officer will be available to assist in further analysis of results if required.

2 Bureau service

Prior to the examination the following procedures should be adhered to:

- The Internal Examiner will undertake training, with the CAA Support Officer, in the use of the OMR system (unless training has been undertaken on a previous occasion).
- The Internal Examiner will inform the Examinations Office of his/ her intention to use the OMR system. This to be done via the Examination Information Sheet and to be undertaken at least eight weeks in advance of the examination session. This will allow the Examinations Office time to schedule OMR exams as early as possible in the Examination Period.
- The Examinations Office will contact the CAA Support Officer with details of OMR examinations. The CAA Support Officer will supply the required number of Student Answer Sheets to the Examinations Office and will supply the Lecturer Answer Sheet and the Batch

Header Sheet, together with an information pack, to the Internal Examiner.

- The Internal Examiner will verbally instruct candidates in the OMR procedure at the final lecture of the Module, using the information pack supplied by the CAA Support Officer. No further instruction, verbal or otherwise, will be given to Candidates in the Examination Hall.
- The Internal Examiner, after seeking advice from the University Disability and Additional Needs Service, will cater for the requirements of any students with disabilities or additional needs taking the examination. Upon request, the Examinations Office will supply Student Answer Sheets for students with learning difficulties and disabilities directly to the Internal Examiner or to his/her department.
- The Examinations Office, on the day of the examination, will supply the Student Answer Sheets for all students, other than students with learning difficulties and disabilities, who will be catered for in accordance with the procedure in Section 1 above.
- Candidates must provide their own pencils and erasers for the examination.

Following the examination, the procedures to be adopted are:

- The Invigilator will collect the Student Answer Sheets at the end of the Examination, checking that they are in good condition (not stapled, tagged, folded, torn etc). Any scripts that are not in good condition should be put to the top of the pile.
- The Internal Examiner will take responsibility for the collection of the OMR Student Answer Sheets from the Examination Hall and for the collection of OMR Answer Sheets from students with learning difficulties and disabilities. (Scripts can be collected from the Examination Halls immediately prior to, or following, a scheduled exam in the same venue. Scripts not collected from the Examination Hall by the end of the Examination Period will be taken to the Examinations Office and may be collected from there.)
- The Internal Examiner will visually check the OMR forms – checking ID numbers are 'coded' in as well as written, that incorrect answers have been erased, that pencil, not biro, has been used, that horizontal lines have been used to indicate the correct answer and that scripts are in good condition. Any scripts which do not satisfy these criteria should be put to the top of the pile and drawn to the attention of the CAA Support Officer when the scripts are brought to Learning and Teaching Development for processing. They will require manual checking after processing.

- The Internal Examiner will then take the Student Answer Sheets, together with the Lecturer Answer Sheet and the Batch header, to Learning and Teaching Development. (See Service Level Statement for hours of service.) A receipt will be issued.
- Learning and Teaching Development will provide a secure system for processing (see Service Level Statement).
- The CAA Support Officer will notify the Internal Examiner as soon as the results are ready for collection. This is normally within five working days from dispatch (see Service Level Statement).

The Internal Examiner is responsible for the hand marking of any Student Answer Sheets rejected by the OMR System and for manually checking any scripts separated out at visual checking.

- The Internal Examiner, or another member of academic staff, should manually check at least five per cent of the OMR scripts.
- The CAA Support Officer will be available to assist in further analyses of results if required.

Service level statements

1 In-house statement example

The following is a description of the service for internal clients. It is intended for use by Computing Services staff and clients. For summative work, the client is normally the Internal Examiner.

Procedure for handling CAA forms

Computing Services are offering the OMR system for marking CAA multiple choice as a 'while-you-wait' system using the following criteria:

1   The client telephones the Computing Services Information Desk to arrange a time to run the forms through the OMR. This will normally be within an hour depending on operator availability. The Information Desk opening hours are 9am–5.30pm Monday–Thursday, 9am–5pm Fridays, except for 2pm–3pm on Thursdays.
2   The client brings the required input to the Information Desk. The operator is called and takes the forms, signing for them in the CAA processing book at the Information Desk.

3   The operator on duty will run the CAA work through the reader and process the results.
4   The client will wait at the Information Desk while the work is done.
5   The client will sign the CAA processing book on receiving the processed results printout, original Student Answer Sheets and floppy disk (if required).

The turnaround time for a test should only be a few minutes – the time needed to physically put the sheets through the OMR and for the reports to be printed.

Required input

For a formative or summative test to be processed, the following are required:

1   A complete set of sheets for each test consisting of:

- a single Batch Header sheet
- a single Lecturer Answer Sheet
- the Student Answer sheets.

2   A blank disk to receive the raw data and text file copy of the reports (if required).

Output

For each test processed, the following will be produced:

1   A set of paper reports comprising:

- student results by student number
- student results in alphabetical order
- student results ranked from lowest to highest
- student results in order of processing
- full results report
- question analysis and test summary report.

2   Two files on floppy disk (if required):

- raw data as output by the OMR
- text file version of the paper reports.

The system is run purely as a processing service. This means that no data will be retained or archived by Computing Services. The service is dependent on the availability of OMR equipment. Computing Services will run a monthly diagnostic test of the OMR equipment.

Feeding forms through the OMR

Forms should arrive in good condition. Forms which are not in a condition adequate for automatic processing will not be processed. Such forms will be kept separately and delivered with the output to the client. If forms fail to be read on the first pass, up to five attempts will be made. The actual number of attempts is at the discretion of the operator. Forms which are rejected due to double feeding or wrong orientation will always be resubmitted. Any urgent problems will be referred to Computing Services Customer Services staff. Other problems will be emailed to the responsible Customer Services staff for logging and consideration.

2 Bureau service level statement example

The following is a description of the service for internal clients; normally the Internal Examiner. It is intended for use by Learning and Teaching Development staff and clients.

Procedure for handling CAA forms

Learning and Teaching Development (LTD) are offering a bureau service for marking CAA multiple-choice questions. Student answer sheets will be marked off-campus by a third party, using the following procedures:

1   The Client gives two weeks' notice to LTD of a test taking place. This allows LTD to give the required two-week notice of a dispatch to the scanning company. This then guarantees the turnaround time outlined in Procedure 7.
2   The Client brings the Student Answer Sheets, Batch Header and Lecturer Answer Sheet to the CAA Support Officer at LTD, between the hours of 9.00am and 12.30pm, Monday–Friday.
3   LTD will issue a receipt.
4   LTD will securely store scripts.
5   LTD will electronically scan answer sheets, prior to dispatch. This is to provide a back-up in case scripts are lost in the post. These

electronic images will be deleted after the original scripts have been returned to the internal examiner.

6   The CAA Support Officer will dispatch the forms to the company. Special delivery or courier service will be used. During term-time a minimum of one dispatch per week will take place. This will be on a Thursday at 12.30p.m. Forms are required to be with LTD by 11.30a.m. on a Thursday for dispatch that day.

7   The scanning company will process forms within three working days of receipt, ie within four working days from dispatch. A database of results will be emailed to the CAA Support Officer and original scripts returned by courier service.

8   The CAA Support Officer will check that all scripts have been returned to LTD.

9   The CAA Support Officer will produce the reports on the fifth working day after dispatch. When there is a large volume of scripts to be processed this may take until the sixth working day after dispatch.

10   The CAA Support Officer will notify the client, by email, as soon as the results are ready. A spreadsheet with results will be attached. Clients will be given the option to collect printed reports and original scripts or for these to be put in the internal mail.

Required input

A complete set of sheets for each test consisting of:

•   a Batch Header sheet/s
•   a Lecturer Answer sheet/s
•   the Student Answer sheets.

Output

For each test processed, the following will be produced:

1   A set of paper reports comprising:

•   student results by student number
•   student results in alphabetical order
•   student results ranked from lowest to highest
•   student results grouped by programme code
•   student results with student responses listed
•   question analysis and test summary report

2   One spreadsheet containing raw and percentage marks and indicating which questions were answered correctly, incorrectly or left blank.
3   Individual student feedback forms, for coursework or diagnostic tests, are available on request.

Feeding forms through the OMR

Forms should arrive in good condition. Forms which are not in a condition adequate for automatic processing will not be processed. Such forms will be kept separately and delivered with the output to the client for manual marking.

Scalability

As the use of optical data-capture CAA increases it is useful to consider the limiting factors affecting how many scripts your optical CAA system can handle in a given time. The scalability of such a system raises a series of questions, including the following:

1   *How fast are the scripts being generated?*   During exam periods a backlog of optical CAA jobs could build up. What is the maximum acceptable delay? What are the security arrangements if scripts have to be kept overnight?
2   *What is the maximum turnaround time?*   Should optical CAA jobs be processed on demand, or only on a specified day each week? If the system is being used for non-assessment purposes (market research, course evaluation forms etc), which jobs have priority? What sort of maintenance contract exists for the hardware and software?
3   *What happens to the scripts between leaving the student and being processed?*   Physical handling of the optical forms should be minimised, especially if they are to be marked by an auto-fed OMR machine. At what point in the process does the lecturer become responsible for the scripts? If dispatching to a bureau, what provision is there should scripts go missing?
4   *What happens to the marks after processing?*   Some reports will be for public consumption, ie published on a noticeboard, but others will be for the lecturer only. To whom are the reports given and how? What happens to the original exam scripts after processing? Are spreadsheets supplied? Are the reports compatible/comparable with those associated with the traditional assessment process?
5   *What are the training needs for key personnel?*   You need several staff

trained to operate the hardware for an in-house system, to allow for illness and absence. Running an OMR will only be a small part of their responsibilities. Running an OMR/OCR/ICR scanner involves a substantial amount of error trapping and this can be time-consuming. Academics may welcome a short workshop giving guidance on putting together questions that may be marked by an optical CAA system. OMR is more versatile than the simple 'tick one of five' style with which it is most commonly associated. OCR and ICR are more versatile still.

6   *How is the operator's time paid for?*   As demand for the service grows, it may become necessary to re-deploy staff, or train up other staff to handle the load. This may become an issue as usage of the optical CAA service grows.

7   *How fast can the whole optical CAA system reliably work in practice?* Never mind what the manufacturers claim, what results do *you* get for a service of the quality and reliability that you need? A fast throughput with many errors takes longer to process than a slower rate with no errors. This applies to both in-house and bureau approaches.

8   *How will you maintain contact with your users?*   This is easy during the pilot phase, because there are so few of them. As the service grows, you may need to formalise a structure for the users to feed back information to you, and for users to gather and talk amongst themselves. (This might be a regular meeting or an email list.)

9   *Does the speed of the scanner have implications for large numbers of scripts?*   Actual physical throughput of the optical scanner itself (number of pages read per second) is not usually an issue. An auto-fed OMR system typically reads 2 scripts per second, and printing the reports on a laser printer takes longer than the computational processing. For example, a test of 47 students generated twelve A4 pages covering all seven of the example reports given. The scanning time of 25 seconds was less than the time it took to print the 12 pages. The service is run as a while-you-wait service, and it takes longer for the scripts to be transported to the computer centre than it does for them to be marked. Dispatches to and from a bureau service and associated administration at each end can take three days. A typical bureau service scanning and processing turnaround will be in the region of three working days. This implies a minimum of six working days in total. Examinations may require multiple dispatches in order to meet both demand and turnaround time to meet deadlines for exercises such as Examination Board Meetings.

Examination Answer Sheet ■ Loughborough University

Student ID

Examination/
Test Title: _____

Date: _____   Seat Number:
(if applicable)

- **Use an HB pencil. DO NOT USE black ink**
- PRINT your student ID Number in the box provided and strike out the appropriate blue box below each digit.
- Enter the details at the top of the sheet. PRINT your Examination/ Test title, Date, Seat Number.
- Make your choices with a horizontal line (joining the dashes on each side of the box). Please make each choice like this:-
- This form will be read by machine. Do not mark in any other way.
- Do NOT mark your choice with ticks, crosses or circles.
- **If you make a mistake, erase it thoroughly.**
- Do not pierce, deform, or attach this form to any other stationery.

	A	B	C	D	E
■ 1.					
2.					
3.					
4.					
5.					
■ 6.					
7.					
8.					
9.					
10.					
■ 11.					
12.					
13.					
14.					
15.					
■ 16.					
17.					
18.					
19.					
20.					
■ 21.					
22.					
23.					
24.					
25.					
■ 26.					
27.					
28.					
29.					
30.					

	A	B	C	D	E
■ 31.					
32.					
33.					
34.					
35.					
■ 36.					
37.					
38.					
39.					
40.					
■ 41.					
42.					
43.					
44.					
45.					
■ 46.					
47.					
48.					
49.					
50.					
■ 51.					
52.					
53.					
54.					
55.					
■ 56.					
57.					
58.					
59.					
60.					

Figure B1   Example of optical input forms for OMR CAA: Examination Answer Sheet

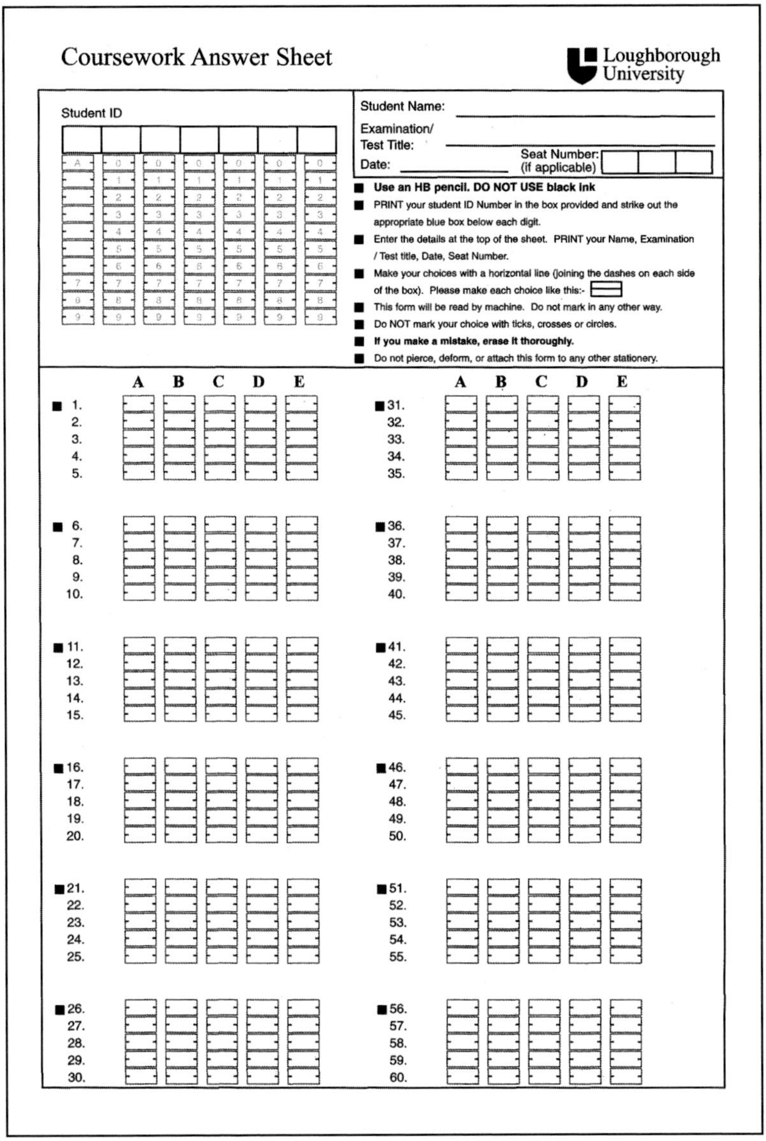

Figure B2 Example of optical input forms for OMR CAA: Coursework Answer Sheet

Batch Header Sheet

Loughborough University

Please mark like this ▭. We recommend using an HB pencil. Do not use black ink.
Mark each response with a horizontal line (joining the dashes on each side of the box).

Lecturer Name   *(Print)* _____

Department   *(Print)* _____

Examination/Test Title *(Print)* _____

Department Code

A A
B B
C C
D D
E E
F F
G G
H H
I I
J J
K K
L L
M M
N N
O O
P P
Q Q
R R
S S
T T
U U
V V
W W
X X
Y Y
Z Z

Module Code

A	0	0	0
B	1	1	1
C	2	2	2
D	3	3	3
F	4	4	4
P	5	5	5
	6	6	6
	7	7	7
	8	8	8
	9	9	9

Date of Test

Day	Day	Month	Year	Year
0	0	Jan	0	0
1	1	Feb	1	1
2	2	Mar	2	2
3	3	Apr	3	3
	4	May	4	4
	5	Jun	5	5
	6	Jul	6	6
	7	Aug	7	7
	8	Sep	8	8
	9	Oct	9	9
		Nov		
		Dec		

MARKING SCHEDULE

Mark for a correct answer: (Default = +4)	Mark for an Incorrect answer: (Default = -1)	Mark for a null response: (Default = 0)
+5	+5	+5
+4	+4	+4
+3	+3	+3
+2	+2	+2
+1	+1	+1
0	0	0
-1	-1	-1
-2	-2	-2
-3	-3	-3
-4	-4	-4
-5	-5	-5

Forms Returned
(Office Use Only)

0	0	0
1	1	1
2	2	2
3	3	3
4	4	4
5	5	5
6	6	6
7	7	7
8	8	8
9	9	9

☐ I have visually checked the input forms for marking-up errors.

☐ I have completed a Lecturer Answer Sheet showing the placement of the correct answers.

☐ I have completed all the details at the top of this Batch Header Sheet.

Place the Batch Header Sheet and Lecturer Answer Sheet on top of the Student Answer Sheets, and return to Learning and Teaching Development.

Tel/Ext No: _____   E-mail: _____

Signature: _____   Date: _____

Figure B3 Example of optical input forms for OMR CAA: Batch Header Sheet

Lecturer Answer Sheet

Loughborough University

Lecturer Name: *(Print)* ______________________________

Department: *(Print)* ______________________________

Examination/Test title: *(Print)* ______________________________

Date: *(Print)* ______________________________

- PRINT the Department, Your Name, Examination/Test Title and Date of the examination in the spaces provided
- This form will be read by machine.
- **Use an HB pencil, and join the dashes on each side of the box.**
- Do NOT mark your choice with ticks, crosses or circles, and do not use black ink.
- **If you make a mistake, erase it thoroughly.**
- Mark each correct answer with a horizontal line (joining the dashes on each side of the box) on the appropriate question line. Please mark your choice like this: -

	A	B	C	D	E		A	B	C	D	E
1.						31.					
2.						32.					
3.						33.					
4.						34.					
5.						35.					
6.						36.					
7.						37.					
8.						38.					
9.						39.					
10.						40.					
11.						41.					
12.						42.					
13.						43.					
14.						44.					
15.						45.					
16.						46.					
17.						47.					
18.						48.					
19.						49.					
20.						50.					
21.						51.					
22.						52.					
23.						53.					
24.						54.					
25.						55.					
26.						56.					
27.						57.					
28.						58.					
29.						59.					
30.						60.					

Figure B4 Example of optical input forms for OMR CAA: Lecturer Answer Sheet

Examination instructions and invigilator's information

This appendix contains an example student computer-based assessment examination instructions and examination invigilator's information. These examples are amended from examination documentation used at the University of Luton. The authors acknowledge the contributions of Rebecca Vafadari and Stan Zakrzewski.

Student examination instructions

Please read all of these instructions before touching the computer.

1   Enter your Examination Identification Number as follows: <three-digit computer seat no.> – <8-figure student ID number> <first 4 characters of surname> eg 005-98765432VAFA

Do NOT put any spaces between the numbers and letters. Put a hyphen between the computer seat number and your student number. Your computer seat number is attached to the top left corner of your monitor. Your 8-figure student ID number is found on your student card.

2   DO NOT PRESS ENTER OR CLICK ON THE 'OK' BUTTON UNTIL YOU ARE TOLD TO DO SO BY A MEMBER OF STAFF.

3   As you go through the test, look at the Test Caption at the top of the screen. It will tell you:

- your username
- the test name
- the current question number
- how many questions you have answered so far out of the total number
- the time remaining

4   To answer a question, use the mouse to drag the cursor to the answer. Click on the answer and the circle next to it will become highlighted. Then drag the cursor to the OK button and click. You will automatically move to the next question.

5   If at any point before you exit the test you wish to change any of your answers, simply click on your preferred answer and the highlighted circle will move to the answer you have chosen. It is important that you then click on the OK button to submit your amended answer.

6   If you do not wish to answer a question straight away, click the OK button and move on to the next question.

7   Keep looking at the Test Caption to monitor your progress through the examination.

8   When you have answered the last question, you will automatically be shown any questions you have not already answered.

9   A message screen will inform you when you have answered all the questions. It will give you the choice of finishing and exiting the examination, or continuing. If you select FINISH you will exit the examination and will not be able to return to it.

10   If you select CONTINUE you can check and amend your answers until the time limit is reached.

The navigation buttons that appear at the top left of the screen are as follows:

| Start of test | Back one question | Forward one question | End of test |

You can use these to move through the test.

11   It is important that once you have selected your answer to a question you submit your answer and move to the next question by clicking on the OK button, NOT BY USING THE NAVIGATION BUTTONS SHOWN ABOVE.

12   Click the RED button at the top left of the screen and then 'Finish' to exit from the examination.

Examination invigilator's information

Please find enclosed:

- instructions for invigilators
- example timetable
- instructions to candidates.

Please return pack to the Examinations Office after each exam with a completed Senior Invigilator's Report Form.

Instructions for invigilators: computer-based examination

1   Prior to the start of the examination

1.1 The senior invigilator is to collect and sign for hard copies (5) of the examinations from the Examinations Office *45 minutes prior* to the scheduled start time of the examination.

1.2 The senior invigilator should meet with technical support staff, security personnel and other invigilators *30 minutes prior* to the start of the examination.

1.3 Assistance will be provided during the examination by technical support staff, but all matters relating to the supervision of the examination and candidates will remain the responsibility of the invigilation staff, under the direction of the senior invigilator.

1.4 Display the unstapled copy of the register(s) provided by the Examinations Office in a prominent position outside the entrance to the exam room. Please ensure that you collect sellotape or Blu Tack from the Examinations Office in order to do this. The stapled copy of the register(s) is to be used to record attendance.

1.5 Ensure a student instruction sheet and checklist is present by each workstation. (Stations to be used will be specified on the registers in the examination pack.)

1.6 The senior invigilator is to ensure that the support staff have tested the system for each examination on selected workstations (also check that the 'Taster' program has been removed).

1.7 The senior invigilator should at this stage familiarise him/herself with the location of the contingency workstations in the examination room.

1.8 The 'Presenter' software will be activated on each workstation by support staff.

2   Commencement of the examination

2.1 When all workstations are ready, candidates may be allowed to enter the room and should be directed to their allocated workstations. Candidates should be requested to remain quiet as they enter the room and find their seats. If a student's name does not appear on any of the registers provided, the student must be sent to the Examinations Office where they will be asked to sign a form accepting responsibility for not being registered on a module. On completing this form, the Examinations Office will tell them which room to go to, and issue them with a pink receipt. If a student produces a pink receipt, allocate a seat number and add their name and reference number to the bottom of the register by hand.

2.2 The senior invigilator should then direct invigilation staff to activate the relevant examination from the 'Presenter' examination menu for each student (ie select the appropriate examination for the candidate at each workstation from the menu screen). It is suggested that each invigilator should be allocated an area within the room of approximately 30 candidates.

2.3 Students should then be requested to enter their Examination Identification Number: <three-digit computer seat no.> – <8-figure student ID number> <first 4 characters of surname> eg 005-98765432VAFA

2.4 It is important that students are told, 'Do not press OK or RETURN', as this will start the examination. If a student presses return, the invigilator should press the RED button (top left corner) then press FINISH. The invigilator should then re-select the examination, as in 2.2 above, and 2.3 is then repeated.

2.5 Student ID cards are checked against the examination ID number entered and the student register provided by the Examinations Office. Each student must be noted as present or absent on the register and the workstation number should also be checked and noted.

2.6 If there is a second examination being taken in the same session, the second group of students are then permitted to enter the room and are seated while the first group's ID numbers are being checked as in 2.5. The examination is selected as above and examination ID numbers are entered.

2.7 Standard invigilation announcements are made to all students by the senior invigilator regarding baggage, mobile phones etc, as per the announcements sheet in this pack.

2.8 Students should be directed to the user instructions and checklist sheet placed by their machines, then requested to read them through prior to the start of the examination.

2.9 Students are instructed to start the examination by the senior invigilator.

3   During the examination

3.1 Students are not permitted to leave the examination room within the first 20 minutes or the last 5 minutes of the examination except where there is an emergency. Where there are two groups taking the same examination but at different times, *the first group are not allowed to leave the examination room until the scheduled completion of the examination for that group.*

3.2 Students arriving up to 20 minutes late should be permitted to commence the examination in the normal manner; however, no additional time is allowed.

3.3 It is essential that the senior invigilator informs Learning Technology staff of the total number of candidates present in the computer room within 15 minutes of the start of the examination and, as soon as possible thereafter, the individual totals for each examination taking place.

4   Contingency arrangements

4.1 If a student has a problem with a workstation that the invigilator cannot resolve unaided, then go to the technical support staff for assistance.

4.2 If there is a crash on an individual workstation within 15 minutes of the start of the examination, the invigilator logs the student out and then the student is logged on to an alternative workstation in the contingency area (full time allowed).

4.3 If the workstation crashes between 15 and 45 minutes of the start of the examination, the student is taken to the Examinations Office where one of the following alternatives will be applied:

- The student is given a hard copy of the examination.
- The student is given the option of taking the examination on a computer in the second group of the examination if there is one. In this instance, the student must remain supervised until the commencement of the examination.
- If sufficient evidence is available to make a valid judgement of the student's performance, then details will be

referred to the Board of Examiners, who will make their decision based on the evidence available.

4.4 If a crash occurs 45 minutes or more after the start of the examination, the student should be taken to the Examinations Office. The answers will be stored in the normal manner and sufficient evidence will normally be available for the Board of Examiners to make a valid judgement of the student's performance.

4.5 If the whole server collapses, the examination should be rescheduled using the re-sit paper, unless the crash occurs 45 minutes or more after the start of the examination and sufficient evidence exists to make a valid academic judgement of the student's performance.

4.6 If any answer files are lost, the standard University procedures for lost scripts are followed.

5   On completion of the examination

5.1 When the examination is complete, all the students are reminded to ensure they have clicked the RED button at the top left of the screen and have then pressed the FINISH button.

5.2 Students are requested to leave the examination room quickly and quietly as there may be a second group waiting to come in. Students should be discouraged from congregating immediately outside the main entrance to the examination room, as this will cause congestion and confusion for any second group. It is important that where the second group consists of further students taking the same examination, the senior invigilator must ensure there is no contact between the two groups.

5.3 The senior invigilator is required to complete a senior invigilator's report form for each sitting of the examination, noting any incidents which have occurred. The total number of students attending each examination within each sitting must be clearly noted on the appropriate senior invigilator's report.

5.4 When the examination is complete (where there are two groups then this is when both groups have finished), the senior invigilator form(s), with the completed register(s) for the examination session must be returned to the Examinations office.

5.5 It is essential that ALL completed and/or unused hard copies of the examination are returned and signed in to the Examinations Office.

5.6 A list report of results, analysis and answer files on disk will be available for collection, with the completed registers, from the Examinations Office the following day.

6   Example timetable of activities

6.1 Students are normally to attend 15 minutes prior to the scheduled start of the examination. During this time, candidates should be
directed to their workstations. Activities should then be conducted in
accordance with the following timetable.

Examination session (eg morning, afternoon and evening)

Group one (L)
8.30	Senior invigilator reports to the Examinations Office
9.00	Students arrive
9.15	Registration (2.2–2.8)
9.30	Start answering questions (2.9)
9.30–10.30	Examination in progress (3.1–4.6)
10.30	Finish examination (5.1–5.2)

Group two (M)
10.30	Students arrive
10.45	Registration (2.2–2.8)
11.00	Start answering questions (2.9)
11.00–12.00	Examination in progress (3.1–4.6)
12.00	Finish examination (5.1–5.2)
12.10	Senior invigilator returns completed senior invigi-lator's report forms, registers and hard copies to Examinations Office

Invigilator's instructions to candidates: computer-based examinations

Before allowing students to enter the exam room

Ensure registers are put up outside the exam room entrance. Remind all
students to check their seat number before entering the exam room. Ask
students to get ID cards ready, as this helps the security check. If a
student's name does not appear on a register, follow instructions in 2.1. If
more than one exam is taking place, enter the largest group first.

Once students have entered the exam room

Please read out the following instructions to the candidates before the
start of each examination:

1   Please ensure you are sitting at the desk you have been allocated. If you have any problems with that machine, please raise your hand.

2   Enter your computer seat number (normally fixed to the computer monitor), followed by a hyphen, then your student reference number, followed by the first four characters of your surname, eg 005-98765432VAFA.

3   DO NOT PRESS OK OR RETURN
     (Request that invigilators check ID cards against students' entries and registers. If applicable instruct second group to enter room.)

4   All bags, coats, mobile telephones (switched off) and other personal items must be left at the back of the room. Money, keys and credit cards must be kept about your person. You will not be permitted access to any such bags during the examination. Please make sure that any notes or books you have with you are left in the baggage area.

5   Please ensure your ID card is placed where it can be seen clearly by the invigilator.

6   If the fire alarm sounds you will be instructed to stop writing and must await further instructions.

7   You must not take out any rough working, unused examination stationery or other materials.

8   If you are found with unauthorised material you could be subject to disciplinary procedures which may result in immediate termination of your studies at this University.

Example staff development programmes

Designing and using objective tests

Programme

10.00	Welcome and introductions
10.15	Background to objective tests
	• definitions
	• current use in higher education
	• ways of using objective tests
10.45	Question types
11.15	Designing questions and tests
12.00	Feedback and scoring
12.20	Discrimination and facility
12.30	Test structure
12.45	Discussion
13.00	Close of workshop

Computer-based assessment workshop

Programme

13.30	Welcome and introduction
13.40	Computer-based assessment: an overview
	• definitions
	• current use in higher education
	• examples of CBA materials currently available
	• demonstration of software
14.30	Case study: an institutional computerised assessment system

14.50   Case study: alternatives to objective testing – an expert system for project, self and tutor assessment

15.05   Pedagogical issues and guidelines for implementation

15.30   Tea/coffee

15.45   Discussion

16.25   Evaluation

16.30   Close of workshop

Model for the implementation of screen-based assessment

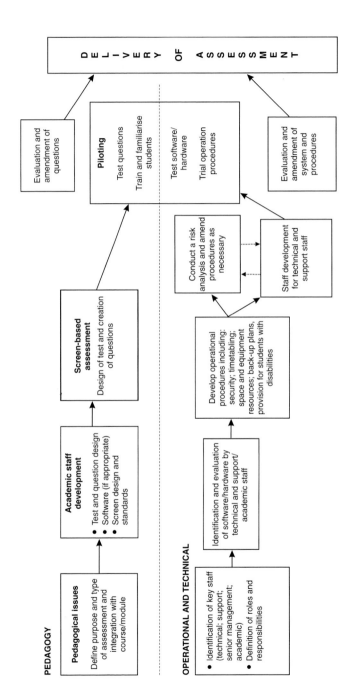

PEDAGOGY

Pedagogical issues

Define purpose and type of assessment and integration with course/module

Academic staff development

- Test and question design
- Software (if appropriate)
- Screen design and standards

Screen-based assessment

Design of test and creation of questions

Evaluation and amendment of questions

Piloting

Test questions

Train and familiarise students

Test software/ hardware

Trial operation procedures

Conduct a risk analysis and amend procedures as necessary

Staff development for technical and support staff

Evaluation and amendment of system and procedures

DELIVERY OF ASSESSMENT

OPERATIONAL AND TECHNICAL

- Identification of key staff (technical; support; senior management; academic)
- Definition of roles and responsibilities

Identification and evaluation of software/hardware by technical and support/ academic staff

Develop operational procedures including: security; timetabling; space and equipment resources; back-up plans, provision for students with disabilities

Figure E1 Initial planning and development

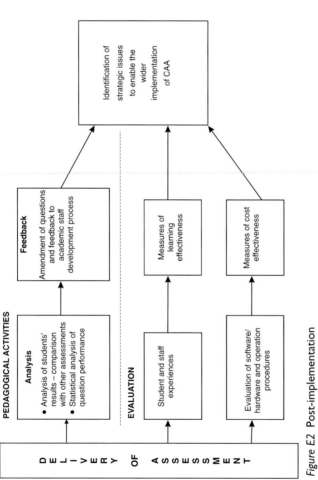

Figure E2 **Post-implementation**

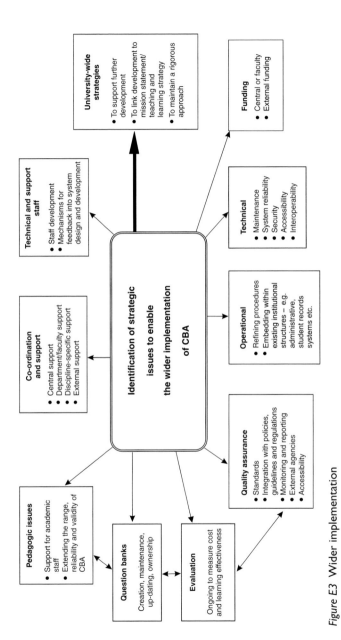

Figure E3 Wider implementation

Index